808s & Otherworlds

Memories, Remixes, & Mythologies

SEAN AVERY MEDLIN

Two Dollar Radio
Books too loud to ignore

"Like the light of an event horizon, this work races toward and struggles against the gravity of Blackness. Lovechild of Sun Ra and Sailor Moon, Sean Avery Medlin sings into the narrow space between hope and rage, bridging political and pop culture galaxies. If our suburbs have become burnt-out satellites circling a world long lost to racism, this book is our S.O.S., transmitting radio waves for searchers and survivors. What an expansive and timely poetic voice!"

—AMAUD JAMAUL JOHNSON, AUTHOR OF *RED SUMMER*, *DARKTOWN FOLLIES*, AND *IMPERIAL LIQUOR*

"In this small book, Medlin's words pack a punch. If you're already familiar with him, you will enjoy catching up to his latest thoughts. If you (like me) are new to his world (Hip Hop) but want to hear what he has to say about issues surrounding BLM and Black culture, just dive into his prose—short bits and poetry meant to evoke an understanding by immersing us in his memories, experiences and observations. I think you'll get a new view of the world from these pages."

—LINDA BOND, AUNTIE'S BOOKSTORE (SPOKANE, WA)

Two Dollar Radio
Books too loud to Ignore

WHO WE ARE Two Dollar Radio is a family-run outfit dedicated to reaffirming the cultural and artistic spirit of the publishing industry. We aim to do this by presenting bold works of literary merit, each book, individually and collectively, providing a sonic progression that we believe to be too loud to ignore.

TwoDollarRadio.com

Proudly based in
Columbus
OHIO

@TwoDollarRadio

@TwoDollarRadio

/TwoDollarRadio

Printed in Canada

SOME RECOMMENDED LOCATIONS FOR READING *808S & OTHERWORLDS*:
During long car rides to neighboring cities, on a bed, chair, or sofa in the morning, at night by a stereo playing *PeteStrumentals*, with friends and family who also love rhythm and poetry, or pretty much anywhere because books are portable and the perfect technology!

Book Club & Reade Guide
of questions and topics for discussion is available at twodollarradio.com

PHOTOs→
Nina Paz Photography,
IG: @ninapazphotography

For the world from which I came,
Mom, my source of loveful flames.
I'm grateful for the shine you gave
and every sacrifice you've made.

In loving memory of Thelma Lee White
and Jaiden Torrez, who both know
how necessary it is
to tell their own stories.

Rest in Paradise,
Michael Lassiter.

Here is one internal world, made from drums and otherworlds.

Table of Contents

Record I

new amerika (i) 5

Iggy & Carti (prelude) 7

How To Be A Rapper...9

Money is Temporary..11

Hidden Cloud Remixed...13

Free Pt. I...15

Record II

new amerika (ii) 19

How To Make Trap Music 21

THUGLIFE Contrapuntal 22

Celebration (Ode to Trap Music) 24

FURVA LUX (Black Light) 26

Sun Valley (Shadowboxing) 28

CORPUS MEUM I 31

Free Pt. II 32

Record III

new amerika (iii) 37

Consequence 39

CORPUS MEUM II 41

Hurricane (Storm gives a lecture on the Middle Passage) 42

Darrien's from the Hidden Cloud 44

Curse 45

Blackgirl Rock (Ode to My Sister) 46

Love Poem 48

Record IV

new amerika (iv) 53

Paradox 54

Nobody 56

Love Letter 57

CORPUS MEUM III 58

Consequence (DOOM Ode) 59

Pokedéx Entry #238: Smoochum 61

In Our Dreams 63

Record V

new amerika (v) 67

record of Blackfolk in az 69

Debt 71

Touch 73

CORPUS MEUM IV 75

Reclamation 76

King of Nothing 78

On Sight Contrapuntal 79

Record VI

in amerika 83

R.T.C. (Right to Carry) 86

explorer's pack 88

Battlefront 89

Mr. Popo (Erasure) 91

Hallie 94

Iggy & Carti 96

Suit of Wands 102

CORPUS MEUM V (Afro) 104

What It's Like To Be A Suburban Black Demiboy................107

Excerpts from skinnyblk

The Making of an Album & Play............................108

Power Ranger...110

Tuxedo Mask...113

Hulk..116

Silver Surfer...119

demiboy 123

demiboy reprise 125

Acknowledgements...131

Pieces Previously Appeared in…..............................133

References & Credits...135

We are beast until proved beneficial.
Monsters until proven Monetary.
Danez Smith

I'm the only thing I'm afraid of
Kanye West

808s & Otherworlds

Record I

new amerika (i)

Outside our windshield, heat haze blurs asphalt, stucco homes blur in boiling mist. We cruise, blasting Erykah Badu's *New Amerykah,* passing metal birds on runways and orange-roofed homes along canals, stopping under traffic lights where cars brake and honk. The air-conditioning hums, almost harmonizing with Erykah, her low voice goosebumping my skin more than cold ventilation, *I stay woke* she sings to my Father and me, and I too have longed to stay awake.

After every listen, I have many questions: where are the scaly underwater scientists, who are the children who made themselves invisible, and can I make myself invisible? We live in a new housing development. arizona's suburbia is an oven, we bake beneath blue skies into one amerikan pie. CDs play throughout the car and house stereo morning, evening, and night. Spellbound by music, I hear the question: *what if there was no niggas / only Master Teachers?*

There are no rappers that I relate to. Rappers are hood reporters, and I do not live in the hood. I live in a new housing development. If people who look like me live in the hood, then I am not like people who look like me. I enjoy hood reports though, because they let me ask real questions—like when ~~Mos Def~~ Yasiin Bey raps *F*%K THE EMPIRE*, and I Google search *the empire* on an old desktop Dad gifted me on my 10th birthday, finding the galactic empire from *Star Wars*, but also the dictionary definition of *empire*, and wondering if u.s. military bases overseas are like imperial outposts on other planets, and if so, am I a rebel or an imperial—so I frequent Dad's CD rack in the family room. There are stacks and stacks of rap CDs, an entire library of music, much more interesting than wiry-armed acacia trees holding tufts of green leaves, sitting alone in rock yards with few weeds, maybe an anthill for company. I quickly pick up three things:

1. Boys who look like me cannot be warm. Instead, we must be cool.
2. Many things maintain a Blackboy's cool: luxuries, money, sex.
3. Cool Blackboys are born in trenches; Blackness is a chasm.

I begin to think of Blackgirls, and their place in Hip-Hop music. My Sister would lie down on our carpet and sing hooks while I stuttered through verses. Rarely did we hear girls like her on any part but the chorus, outside of Ms. Lauryn Hill and Erykah. I think of my lost second-grade friend, who Common once called subhuman, bound to be bound by twine and burnt, *in a circle of f*gg*ts / your name is mentioned* Com accuses. I used to sing-along to that lyric, until I found where I am: uncomfortably squished in binaries that blister and buck one's sense of self.

Every reflection of me told the same story: dead, jail, drunk, high, fist, gun, rock, fly. Even Blackstar's "K.O.S." felt more S.O.S. than *B.I.B.L.E*, basic instructions Blackfolks live out eternally. As a young person with one friend of my complexion on the block (whose Dad was also military), I concluded that because the Soulquarians (The Roots crew and usual suspects) said so, it must be true of my folk. Which is to say, I adopted a performance of a performance as my truth; we have inherited a void, and still, we're strip-searched down to the bone, tarred, feathered, and made to dance.

Iggy & Carti (prelude)

Iggy Azalea... holds hands with new "boyfriend" Playboi Carti...

When Iggy & Carti hold hands: my college friend says *I'm not into white guys*,
another *Blacked* video is uploaded, nonBlackgirls tweet *my Black boyfriend said
that I can say nigga,* their boyfriends respond *Blackgirls just jealous*;

    I'm vacuumed back to 2007, my girlfriend is from minnesota, her acne is
    confederate red, which is amerikan red, like the flag my Father works for,
    so I don't question her parents' 6pm curfew, or her gossiping friends,
    always glancing longways, instead I gloat, glad to be marble dark like night
    skies beneath a silver moon, reveling in the chess squares of our skin,
    a dream celebrated in curriculums, which our locked fingers concretize.

        Young Jeezy belts *you know I keep that whitegirl, CHRISTINA AGUILERA,*
        & my girl is indeed a genie in a bottle, a granted wish granting wishes,
        I'm Cory from *Boy Meets World* but I have a 4d curl pattern,
        my Topanga does not have full lips, hers are tight as her mother's eyebrows
        the morning my Father & I knock on her door
        to confess that I ran a few miles that night,
        to lay naked and curious, both of us too afraid to have actual intercourse,
        not because her dad would call me *nigger* but because the unknown is
        simply terrifying,   plus neither one of us know how to put on a condom.

When Iggy & Carti hold hands: I remember most of the cheer-leaders were nonBlack and lightskin, I admired them at lunch from a red gazebo, their nails maroon, their hair strawberry and honey-maple, their suntans more pale than brown paper-bags but never as pale as my girlfriend, whose skin burnt scarlet as the sinner's letter.

I didn't understand the brand we burnished, but I picked the iron myself, while watching tv probably, *Power Rangers*, or something like that, where a whitegirl wears pink, whor-ling pink ribbons.

Paparazzi snap pictures of pop-stars showing affection & I sit on a bus in the 8th grade holding my girlfriend's hand, before her parents order the driver to separate us & ask that teachers stand watch at their doors during passing periods as surveil-lance. I learn to love running away from mirrors; a cold-sweat deadsprint.

Sometime after, I write this poem, wanting to be witnessed.

How To Be A Rapper

Maybe I don't know. Maybe I fumble flows. Maybe one prose poem can't be enough. Some gatekeepers show public bus, handcuffs, potholes, and gang wars as a lyricist's requirements; amerikan gangster roleplayers engulf streams. If this poem is not *How To Be A Rapper*, it is *How To Survive A Multi-Headed, Regenerative Oppressor*—meaning that *rapper* is code for *trickster*. When insulted, rappers insult back quicker than hermes. When instructed, rappers finish both the instruction and the task. Their minds can meld what's given to them: crafting tools to refine their craft's tools.

Some say I'm describing an emcee, there's no difference to me: griot, prophet, poet, all names for the same sleight of mouth. But how to be today's rapper, a decentralized rhyme-saying actor, who appeals to mass media markets and timeline youth culture. Right now rappers are played in the millions, millions and millions of dollars generated. Right now rappers are hot across the globe; right now rappers have power, and power creates callous and generous rulers, cruel to their country's citizens, kind when their kingdom kneels. Rappers buy compounds, sports teams, tanks, snack brands, alcohol brands, energy brands, businesses and properties segregated and resegregated and built and rebuilt on the bodies and mockeries of niggas   cuz niggas make empires.

Anyhow, since I still have your attention, let me share this, you can't say that no one ever told you. To be a rapper is to make repetition, think sledgehammers shaking railroad ties, upside-down heads spinning 360-degrees on crinkled cardboard. Each of these actions require cyclical practice. To be a rapper, then, is to speak, and speak, and speak, until what you say becomes reality.

Money is Temporary

Hip Hop will simply amaze you / Craze you, pay you / Do what-
ever you say do / But... it can't save you.
        "Hip-Hop" by Yasiin Bey f.k.a. Mos Def

no one can tell me that Hip-Hop can't save me /
swear that it made me and daily rap pays me /
rap brought ma baby and she had ma baby
and i bought her louis and fendi and gucci /   ma niggas
still slangin / i told them be bodyguards for me
we're touring in l.a. / i open for Baby and Baby and Bhabie /
i think i feel happy / my canines are icy and shiny and pricey /
ma Momma keeps callin / she saw me on tv but lately
i'm busy with meetings and parties and sessions and press /
smoking and drinking and i'm *not* depressed   *i'm upset* !
my streaming payout is 50K a check ! and that's not enough
to pay off my jet / or my daughter's dog Snoopy's trip
to the vet / or my entourage addiction to xanax and sex /
or the cost of my album / my outfits / my sets / my mortgage /
my lawyer fees piling like stress / and hospital bills /
somethin hurts in my chest / my baby don't text me /
my closest friends and family are dead /
their funerals passed   i'm not really sad /
i really be high and hype and smiling all the time
cuz my bottom teeth blind and my top teeth diamond /
i dropped out and moved out and then i was homeless

and nobody knew me / believed me or saw me /
now i have advertisements on your story /
my left wrist is golden / my right wrist is scabby /
my single is #2 right after Posty / and i need *more* money /
i need more jewelry / i need more luxury foreigns and
i need endorsements /   i don't need therapy /
i need an orgy   i don't need counseling i need a bag !
          i said it before i'm not sad /
sometimes it's just hard to wake up
                    and being famous kinda sucks /
this emergency room   ain't half bad

Hidden Cloud Remixed

Among mountains, where storms roar and clouds cover peaks, there's a whole village'a niggas. In my world we been singin *I wish I could / buy me a spaceship and fly*, but in Otherworld, we did so without buying or dying. Here, we arrived with our culture and our knowledge of weather intact, to prosper secluded and free. Here, we teach our young to command lightning, bend wind and water to their liking, seek their literal higher calling. Here, we did not lose millions to the open sea. Here, there are no prisons or police. Here, Wu-Tang Killa Bees sharpen their freestyle skills while sword-fightin, stuntin like all rappers should.

Tucked off in our own paradise, a country of thunder—autonomous and distant from those asunder—where the fruits of our labors are not for someone else's shelf; if we go to war, we set the terms. Our work and our time is our own, for once. We who weave weapons from discharged electricity of nimbuses, and shape small cities amidst the wisps of stratus clouds, pooling together our power like a fantastic Panther Party! We eat what grows and thrives in the valley thousands of miles below. Our children read books that recount our heritage: from warfare, to wayfarers, to marauders who wrestle us away from rights and homelands, to representatives who rewrite their words and agreements, generations of struggle, succession of riches, crimes, and miracles happening in our community.

Here, we tell the young, the old, the hopeful, the cold, they have the freedom to fly faster than a streak of white heat, simply because us Black sky-splintering folks can!

Free Pt. I

my MAGA hat is signed 🔥 🔥 🔥 🔥 🔥
       Kanye Omari West

When you tweeted that, I thought it was a joke. Kanye MAGA red? No. Kanye white-light of Black plight, not white-knight of new reich. Kanye red-hot soul chops, not blood-red skull opp. Kanye say *bush don't like Black people*, not *racism doesn't exist anymore*. Kanye rap *racism still alive they just be concealin it*, whose mans is on TMZ live with this bullshit?

We believed you was makin music to change the culture, and bring it back to our roots, now you dissin our ancestors and burnin trump's brand in our youth. My students ask
is it true? Did Kanye really fly the coop? I sigh *yes, he's out of view, guess that's what money does to you.*

Me and the homies used to swear by you, Lu', and Lil Weezy Ana. Now Fiasco's unsung, while you and Wayne banter on a syndicated show about racism's wilting, as if you both did not see new orleans drowning; slews of nonBlack artists taking dozens more Grammys, disrespecting your craft over a crowd's constant clapping. I look toward the two of y'all, and wonder if it's the money, or something you've always believed.

Record II

new amerika (ii)

I begin to study rappers on tv because Dad has prohibited the radio, but not BET. I start coming into the family room whenever he is watching *Rap City, Tha Basement*. One episode, Cam'ron wears a pink long-tee, pink bucket hat, pink durag, and black jeans. He's counting money as he's freestyling at the mic, his chain a grandfather clock face on a wire. *My AK was my a.k.a. before my ABC's had me A-OK!* he brags. No, I did not understand those freestyle lyrics as a child, but now his boasts about childhood harlemite soldiering are useful to process moments of my experience.

Seeing Cam with Dipset, thumbing large bills, reminds me of a time I counted bills quadruple my age, which my Uncle produced from a shoebox underneath his bedframe in that old, hilly mining town. *Keep some of it*, he says, passing cash from the pile to my small palm. As I turn to leave the room, Dad walks in with a tense smile and puzzled eyes. *Oh, I was just givin him some cash, a little gift for my nephew*, and Dad says to me *don't take that money*. I hand the bills back. Unc gives Dad a look I'll someday learn as *come on*, *bro*, grinning with passive sharpness. My feet shuffle in compliance with a push from Dad that directs me out the door. By the time I fly home, I forget all about Uncle's room, but rap music sparks these memories. Half a dozen years later, give or take, Shawn Carter drops a movie-packaged ode to bootstrap origin stories and "Blue Magic" heroin, *American Gangster*.

The celebratory lines *thanks to the duffle bag / the brown paper bag / the Nike™ shoebox for holding all this cash* place me back behind Unc's shoulder, his muscle shirt tightening as his arm swipes aside a bedskirt, revealing a small fortune.

When I first hear "P.I.M.P.," three Blackmen stand in piercing sunshine shafted by family room blinds. I'm by Dad's armchair, on linoleum flooring, watching. Every image hangs a moment longer than it plays: 50 seems massive, a tattooed Hulk in a wife-beater, with a loud superhero logo of a chain lying across his neck. There are three Blackwomen on the screen with him, all wearing white, their hands resting soft on 50's arms and shoulders. These women model lingerie, strut smooth like slow pendulums, legs toned thigh to toe. *No cadillacs no perms you can't see / that I'm a muthaf*%kin P.I.M.P.* and I don't know what that means. When Snoop Dogg appears in the video as the chosen one, named by the "PIMP Legion of Doom," my cousins burst into laughter. One giggles *why's he talkin like that?* The other answers *cuz he's a P.I.M.P.!* Dad is silent, focused on the tv, smirking and almost scowling. I imagine myself inside the tv, a chain dangling from my neck, women massaging my back.

This is (Black)manhood, I think, although I'm sure I don't consciously think those words, the message is clear, imprinted on my psyche. If I am to be of worth to this world, there's many things I must first acquire.

How To Make Trap Music

turn up gunshots / plug-in melodyne /
bridge the noise between being shot
and discovering the wound / compress
a dopeboy's ambition with 808 drums /
remember / someone died for these 16s /
introduce the verse with tire screeches /
build brand-new / fresh-out-the-box kicks /
smoke strong the whole studio session /
for inspiration / study sirens as symphonies /
record kitchen appliances for snares / sample
local evening news / *14 shot in 48 hours* /
Notorious Downtown Drug House shutdown /
lay the hook like a trap / once heard / no escape /
test the track at a strip club / test the track again
at another strip club / add the producer's tag /
youtube search *how to make hi-hat triplets* /
make a Soundcloud account / upload weekly /
watch a docu-series on crack cocaine in atlanta /
blast the mastered track / remember / 25 to life
without parole is the minimum sentence
for those who are arrested living this song /
lastly / visit any university / peep what's blaring
from a whitekid's car window as they drive by
in vehicles with license plates that inmates press /

trap hits echo across yards / college / prison / etc /
if your music plays there / start over from the top

THUGLIFE Contrapuntal

i tried to be bourgeoisie / shiny watch and college tee /   Screamin "F*%K THE POLICE !"

looking down at men i see on BET and twitter feeds /   as I ride through the night streets

loving my body is hardly easy / i'm sorry Momma   Swore I saw the devil

degrees cannot save me / boys who look like me   in my empty glass of Hennessy

bleed out on the asphalt / media says it's our fault /   A single witness screamin

tellin us we deserve shots / like boards born for darts /   "Bloody murder / murder !"

justice is not for all of us / not all with 9-5 shifts /   It's a crazy world full of sin

not every student / parent / child / human /   If you play the game /

justice belongs to whiteness / meaning there isn't justice /   you play to win only power to choose whose life ends / *Two Glock four-fives /*

policemen with magnums make my people phantoms / *time for survival*

we pray with hands up for jammed handguns / *Death to my rivals*

once it was me facing an officer's weapon / *Stupid coppers tried to play us out*

but i drove away / and like 2pac sang / *Thug for Life / I will be*

the hate u give little infants f*%ks everybody / *A life of crime I will lead*

cops in uniform are amerika's most dangerous gang / *Listen / you can hear it — the ballad of a dead soldier*

Celebration (Ode to Trap Music)

remember ronald reagan / Jazz in harlem
and Black hipsters refusing to be like everyone else /
uplift independent-out-your-car-trunk record sales /
bless the blue-collar workers dreaming amerika /
consider red-lined areas / the Blues and the deep south /
salute the Black Mafia Family for storming settler states
coke white / hail Colombians and cartels for business /
thank the tastemakers / dancers who ride storms of cash
and cristal / see feds and cops who supply red-dot sights /
praise pyrex / spoons / pots /

honor Anansi the Spider for catching hornets
by emptying his water gourd over their nest / and yelling
it's raining ! quick ! get inside my empty gourd !
then webbing the gourd shut /

thank (in no particular order) /
Jay *Young Jeezy* Jenkins
Kevin *Coach K* Lee
Radric *Gucci Mane* Davis
Nayvadius *Future Hendrix* Wilburn
Tauheed *2Chainz* Epps
1974 atlanta mayor, Maynard Jackson
the Roland TR-808 drum machine
Big Meech

Southwest T
Lexus *Lex Luger* Lewis
Joshua *Southside* Luellen
Xavier *Zaytoven* Dotson
Jonathan *Lil Jon* Smith
the Real Rick Ross
the Dungeon family
Outkast
Leland *Metro Boomin* Wayne
and the city of atlanta for naming itself *the city too busy to hate* /

thank the tenacity and indomitable spirit of African descendants /
celebrate musicians without academic instruments /
bouncing bass / kick / snare / and beats per minute /
beware the military-man in a suit /
who appeared to a group of Blackboys one day /
opened his briefcase / and showed them
blue dollar bills tied with red rubber bands /

FURVA LUX (Black Light)

I'ma rockstar

Symere Bysil Woods, professionally known as Lil Uzi Vert

Plum purple dreads shake like pythons from the scalp of our protagonist. He stands aglow, lit by neon jewels, weapons at the waist of designer denim, ready to battle our Father.

How did we get here? The Light-Bringer's vanity like peacock plumage, warbound with big guns and music emitting from foreign chariots, shadow angels streaking through exhaust smoke, armored immortals faithful to him as youth are to the piper—drawn like flies to phosphorus trap, each 808: bubbles of lava, melodies: molten streams, adlibs: veiny channels, the chorus: a curtain of fire, hot shit as results of self-discovery—Lil Uzi, too short to box with God so he's shooting, the Morning Star ultraviolet and violent!

Soon, he'll become one light amongst hundreds, falling for seven nights until he and his army crash. Crestfallen and zealous, the son of Dawn himself will sink into the shape of a serpent, sliding into paradise, transmuting his diamond grillz into fruit, which two humans will eat to realize their barenaked bodies.

This happened long ago, before a bronze man with hair like wool performed miracles, before a tower or bull challenged our Lord, a rapper did, with tattooed skin, face piercings, fuschia locs like the syrup in his cup, and starlight for teeth.

Before free will was dreamed of, he steamrolled beyond the fixed heavens, pioneering ego and self. Lil Uzi Vert, pridesick rockstar, stood before his Maker and said,

I too deserve to be praised.

Sun Valley (Shadowboxing)

where you from son ?
the sun / son / skin dark like a total eclipse sun / ain't got it
tatted but my city in my skin son / it ain't pretty it's gritty / keep
it real son /

where you really from ?
i'm from the burbs son / thought you never feel flames like this
sun / 8-0-8 bass breakin outta subwoofs / cul-de-sac shakes
smooth off asphalt /

okay you rock like that ?
on 7th with the homies many fridays past / before every corner
had a full-time badge /
we hand out CDs by food-stalls & weeds / Bird   City
cyphers   give me wings /

so you concrete / or stucco ?
i'm three-bedroom home / out west / where ole cotton fields
still grow / Mom drove us east cuz poetry's my green rose / ain't
a mic in avondale for a lauerate ta hold /

sounds like a whole lotta cappin
look / i don't seek validation for rappin / i use to / now i just spit for the passion / for Andrew & John writin verses in heaven / for the child that i was / actin like western projections of Blackness /

whatever you say / are you done yet ?
naw i'm just beginnin / i do it cuz the mayor & police chief are villains / i do it cuz the prosecutor exercise discretion / i do it for my niggas / my Sister my Dad / my cousins / i do it for the niggas left outta history class / i do it for the future & the present & the past /
even though i'm not a Sun Valley native / niggas in the desert since spaniards invaded / we keep livin where our ancestors didn't / we wish the southwest would be different / still ignored / isolated & imprisoned / children of sharecroppers who survived migration / i'm connected to the mountains & mirages / black as the sunset side of South Mountain /

it's so hot in the city folks can't breathe / water on the street but it's all make-believe / get your groceries in the strip-mall by the bank / stop by Circle K / get a lil drank /
i don't mean brown or white / you will need electrolytes / cuz the sunlight burn ya brain /   most work all week & don't get a break   dreamin of a beach just to get away /

landfills swallow anything crossing the Rio /   if you been south then you just know / nothin's really poppin but cuffs & bones / children & adults who call the valley home / stolen land owned by those who only visit the desert to dodge snow / yo ! what if it's returned to those who named it first ? O'odham earth births more resilient souls / yo even though i'm not a Sun Valley native / niggas in the desert since spaniards invaded / we keep livin where our ancestors didn't / we wish the southwest would be different / still ignored / isolated & imprisoned / children of sharecroppers who survived migration / i'm connected to the mountains & mirages / black as the sunset side of South Mountain /

is that everything that you have to say ?

hol' up   Sean Ave heatwave like a sunny day
aye !   peace !

CORPUS MEUM I

my body be the finances of empires /
    old as Greasy Mountain /
    black as the mountain's backside
    at dawn / older than star studies and
    gods / my body both built and builder /
    countries stand because we bent /
my body royal *we* / arisen demigod
    phaeton / the sunbringer / a boy
    thought to be relic & fertilizer /
my body / darkfleshed bluefire / i sing
my body's song / throat like whittled wings / praise
my body / learn to coax their needs
    until the quivers quit / i remember our first
    sprint / how even then / i mistook miracle
    for meaning / how even now / i give myself
    mercy / i give myself forgiveness

Free Pt. II
after Jasmine Mans

400 years of slavery sounds like a choice
      Kanye Omari West

Celebrity is a ghost town. I can't deny that you are free or ill—
white marble floors, calabasas, paris, glasgow, lonely heartsore
son of Black academia—chasing spirits like a moth chases flame.

I love you like boys who grew up Black as me in the burbs, my
day 1's and play cousins. We never dreamed of growing up and
being you. A star is not a sun without planets in orbit, and we
orbited you like moons. You, diamond-cased name-brand deity
of Otis Redding and Chaka Khan samples, rap fanboy turned *it*
boy, multimillionaire by marriage and major record sales, collec-
tor of awards along mansion walls.

We can't tell you nothin, nah, but we can tell that yo money ain't
right; money got you believin there was an option other than the
ship, or the jaws of a shark, got you thinkin whip, fist, rope, and
poplar tree were not the only destinations besides house or field,
got you forgettin enslaved Africans were born and raised on
plantations, sold, rented, or freed by death off plantations, got

you blankin on written passes enslaved folk needed just to leave plantations, got you slow to state the police state is an evolution of 19th century slave catchers—why get yo money right just to get yo history wrong?

Who are we without our ancestry, Ye? Who are you without the musicians you resurrect through samples? How can you say race doesn't matter anymore when the media won't acknowledge your mental wellness, but will empathize with white nationalist shooters? You were right about one thing: *no one man should have all that power.* You are mortal after all, not a G/god, or the son of one. You are your Momma's Blackboy, from chicagoland, who rapped and made soul beats until the world took notice.

Who would've guessed what idol-worship and riches could draw out of you. Your world is so distant from mine, I fear you can't hear me even if you heard this, but Kanye, I hope you live to remember the immeasurable strength our grandest parents had, and the sacrifices they made to survive. What more can we ask of those who risked it all for our chance to be? We hold them in flesh and spirit; we are their wildest dreams.

Record III

new amerika (iii)

Dad's favorite superheroes are my favorite superheroes. He and
I sit in front of the tv watching *Silver Surfer* together. Every epi-
sode opens with the Surfer riding his board through star-speck-
led cosmos. He wears nothing. His loins are smooth. His body,
the same sterling as his board. I want to be like the Silver Surfer:
brilliant, free, diamond, not boy or girl, not dark as charcoal
put on a grill, or white as marker boards in classrooms—not
superstar, bus driver, or drug-dealer—just light tracing letters
that spell my name across the black canvas of space.

Dad watches *Silver Surfer* with me, but his childhood favorite
is *The Incredible Hulk*. He buys me the video game *Hulk* for
Playstation 2. I love it. I get to run around a city, smashing any-
thing and anybody bold enough to exist. Rage is hypnotizing.
The old tv in my room is a portal leading away from avondale to
anywhere, and I'm mad. I don't know why, but I'm mad.

At school, my best friend and I make a blond boy cry because
we tell him God doesn't exist. He's crying into the corn on his
paper lunch tray. There's a student bible on the bookshelf in
my family room. I know the stories of Noah and the flood, of
Moses and the bush. I wonder where Moses and Noah are now,
why there's no one to save the people I hear Erykah sing of,
holdddd onnnn / my people.

Back home, I pause *Hulk* after crushing and splitting a two-
door sedan into boxing gloves. I grab my student bible to verify
the story of Moses: his people led to the promised land, out

of the Pharaoh's regime. I flip pages for illustrations, and see a bearded white man walking up a dune, young and old folks behind him. I find the story of Noah, and there's a picture of a ship rocking on swelling waves. I wonder why God saved so many animals and people, but not my people. Erykah does not ask God, she just sings, and I wish I could sing. I wish all sorts of things: that I was older, louder, that I was not small and separated from my people, that I did not live in avondale, arizona, where no one looks like me.

At school, my best friend and I are two of four Blackboys. There's a fight in the bathroom between one Blackboy and my best friend. They don't like each other; they're mad and I never ask why. I'd rather play-fight at recess as *Dragon Ball Z* characters, with my best friend, the whiteboy we made cry, and a half-Koreanboy also from an air force family.

Putting the student bible back where it belongs, I go into my room, unpausing *Hulk*. I am right where I left off, with my newly made steel boxing gloves. I punch through downtown until the helicopters come, and then I punch through them, too.

Consequence

Let's build a temple, the men said. Let's name it the TRAP. Here, we'll name ourselves—etch our faces into the mountains—we lost all we knew in the stomach of a ship, the teeth of a shark, but let's build a temple. Let's name it the TRAP. This land will recognize our new names, this country that robbed us will sing our song, the capitol will give us capital and we will not work as servants in their cathedral.

I was brought to the TRAP as a child. I gave it my body: it gave me power. Inside, boys offer their tender hearts to gas stoves, the face of their father and their father's father float, suspended like smoke caught in amber. I chose what the grandsons, great-grandsons and great-great-grandsons of slaves choose: to be a ghost of myself—embalmed corpse, and currency commander—to chain the world within feverish finger length because, why not us?

A master orders lessers, makes and unmakes laws, buys humans wholesale, splits families, seas red with blood—master owns what I see and if not master takes what eyes see—we are made of the same stuff, master and I. Flesh, bone, a hole of ash like an urn where the heart was. Let's build a temple, the men said, a place of worship, big, white buildings. Let's name it the TRAP. Here, we'll exchange our skin for gold and gemstones. Here we are Kings.

The cost of power is living in a coffin. It's comfortable, all the meat and liquor one can crave, caked into six sides. Boys walk through the front door of the TRAP and girls go down the cellar door. Boys leave with cold weapons, one long scar, and girls leave with their face frozen like petrified wood. The faces of our fathers say everything is as it should be. Sometimes a boy sees his mother nod in agreement, her face unfossilized for a price.

I hear women breaking themselves out of the TRAP. Is it too late? Can I lift the wooden lid hiding my face? Here is the temple Blackmen built. Our splendor canvassing the Blackwomen we've buried to touch the sky. I'm banging my fist against the hexagon; I'll give power back to break out this prison. I push and punch, the TRAPdoor budges millimeter by millimeter. A smell punctures the mildew, and I know that I'll die here, underground, pushing out.

CORPUS MEUM II

Why is this body marked and named nothing I name myself?
Man is a fragile fort hiding secrets. *Boy* is a seed. *Black* is decaying. No one sees me and says *Dreaming Sunbeam.* I walk like my
Father, cope like him too; poems alarm, alerting who knew. Why
am I quiet when poison seeps in my skin?

I am not a butterfly un-cocooning. I am a boy who is now a man
who was neither all along and more: unknown matter at its melting point: endless seas of thunderclouds. *MY BODY MY BODY.*
Sounds better than skinnyblk, cheeks, nail-beds, dandruff, hair,
dry scalp.

My ancestors were property of propertied white men, labor
to be traded and bartered like tokens. I know too much about
tokens, my value legibly stretched across bone, teeth, stripped
and lathered with grease,   savage   athlete
          gangster   beast. Both currency and investment.
Concurrently an investment.

I miss childhood; I didn't even believe in gender, but Father
stood and stared like stone, and Mother gave a sweet smile like
there was no sickness. Older boys on the block claimed that
a boy's soft spot became a pencil, and that a girl's soft spot
became a sharpener. I thought *how painful love must be, how men
and women must suffer so much.*

Hurricane (Storm gives a lecture on the Middle Passage)

Mutant comes from the latin word *mutare*, meaning to change. In this way all living things are mutants: seeds change into infants, infants change into adults, adults change into compost. What makes superhuman mutants different is that we are aware we are mutants. Therefore we *change* much more than ourselves.

My birth name is Ororo Munroe. Perhaps in another timeline my hero name was *Rain Daughter* or *Flower Mother*, maybe *Water Bearer* or *Desert Savior*, but in this timeline my mutation *changed* into something destructive by definition, a natural act of cleansing and chaos. I wonder if this sort of genetic alchemy has a trigger.

Perhaps some Africans lost in the ocean were mutants, and upon descending the depths, they *mutated* into something not mutant or human. Perhaps having been from my birth-coast, their initial powers were weather phenomena—maybe just a few of them or maybe most of them. These West African mutants could be the eyes fixing wind and water on drylands and cities, mournful ghosts, spinning storm after storm like spin tops crashing into whatever unsunken earth lies ahead; phantoms singing ancestral pain like sea gods seething thunderous waves!

Perhaps these freedom-seeking folks even adapted to their waterworld, becoming more like Namor and the Atlanteans, but dark as cooled lava, and the crowns of orca whales. Who's to say these Mer-Africans don't live deeper than Atlantis or military submarines, deeper than any human, mutant, or cosmic deity can descend. Imagine living on our blue planet, yet dozens of miles below emperors and borders, completely free from tyrannies that rot even superhumans right here on the surface.

Darrien's from the Hidden Cloud

and the cop couldn't tell, despite his sword's hilt hanging from his waist like newsprint paper in the breeze, and his hand, hummingbird-hovering just within reach. Witnesses claim the suspicious officer drew his weapon and shouted *FREEZE, OR I'LL BLOW YOUR F*%KING HEAD OFF*, and Darrien swiveled into stance, standing stiller than a mountain's peak. There was a sound that left the sky too empty to be a gunshot, hot bursts of blue light waves, and a bright, blinding flash. One boy, watching from across the strip mall, said that once he could see again, the cop's pistol lay split on the sidewalk, cut evenly down the barrel in two pieces, as if the firearm had dotted lines, and Darrien, scissors. News reporters say neither Darrien Hunt, nor his family, could be found for comment. Anyone tracking them down for testimonies won't get far, unless they fly without planes, but this is all speculation, especially if you're hearing this and you're not raincloud Black. Matter fact, if you ain't a nigga, and you're hearing this now, you heard *nothing* from me.

Curse

to be us   you must lose whom you love the most /
our potential grows from pain like a pavement rose /
       witness light fading from one's eyes with your own
       and mourn your pupils morphing into kaleidoscopes /

our curse of hatred   our nation hates us /
black flame and phantoms   black operations /
we fought as allies   we pledged with hands high /
yet we're enemies   yet we're killed like thieves

but you still desire   what my family inherits /
power and sorrow   war's vainglorious merits /
       you must be ready to carry and grieve   cycles of death /
       in exchange for celestial strength   show me
       whom you love so much   you sing their name sanctuary /

and you'll be severed from them forever so that you know
my family /
how misunderstood we are   our love / birthplace and
graveyard /
histories that bring sweet joy   and suffering sharp enough
for swords /

Blackgirl Rock (Ode to My Sister)

When you're in the pit, and the breakdown slams you into a snarling wall of hard teeth and fist, or when you're at a party, and racial slurs crack louder than beer bottles, I am with you.

When people who look like you, even family, frown or laugh at you, your piercings and wardrobe, or when you stand stock still as your lover's pink lips slide across yours in public, and bystander glares are burning crosses on proverbial yards—when you're the darkest person in concert photos, when you cry at night because jokes cut like razors on exposed skin, when you stare in mirrors at African cheekbones, and a nose second only in size to your singing voice—I am with you.

* * *

Both you and I know what it is to grow up dark in litchfield park, arizona: where folks who tan easy burn their pale skin, and folks with melanin wish for lightskin; where neighbors stare through you like sound through stucco walls, and classmates pass like you're some ghost haunting loggia halls. Some of them like us too much. Some of them don't give a fuck. We feel like rock-stars, or unkempt weeds in rock lawns. We survived how we did, turned loneliness to rage, mad at the place we live in, and these bodies we're given.

If you cannot see your reflection and think deserving—human, loving lover loved and wondrous brownskin miracle of moon-bright eyes, child of two survivors, two Blackfolks who escaped one thing to persist in the face of another, your mind wide as the desert you did not choose to grow in, but grow in regardless—then hear me. You are more than the pain you have painted, more than the scars you have sown, more than the hurting you've handed to those who only wished to hold you. Look, now, upon your shining reflection. You are beautiful. *You are your best thing.*

I love your middle finger, your natural hair, your weave, wig, locks, braids, and extensions; I love how you scream and slam-dance in living rooms; I love how you talk—please keep living your loud truth—and wherever you are, remember that you are worth more than blood diamonds and 24 karats, you are worth more than oil, and never forget, that I am with you.

Love Poem

I first saw the divine feminine in the poise of a Blackboy's chin,
fixed on high like a moonlit sky, brown eyes beaming down the
bridge of his brown nose, princess pensivity splitting my fore-
head, piercing my temples.

I belong to him as shield belongs to knight, as knight does to
Queen—he is both my princess & Queen in this childhood play-
time we dream. When no adults overlook us outside, we invert
the roles they demand we memorize. A truly Black thing we
did, he and I, with master(s) not looking we dove deeper inside
ourselves; found proof of what makes us shine, feel, real, alive,
still   divine—

& if my Blackboyfriend was my goddess /
I ask not who I am / but only to know
eternally who *she* is / forever and ever /
Blackfem

* * *

My Creator /
There's no limit to what you can do
& many marvels unattributed to you /
who remakes the reprinted blueprints of cool
we use to define ourselves beyond what we do /

who calculated the distance between a gas giant
& one of its moons / who sowed & embroidered
the flag of a nation built on her servitude /

who led a party for self-defense against a country's
counter intelligence / who works five days a week
& still takes loans from the bank / using her savings
to ensure her Daughter gets a college diploma /
who throws the first brick / who heads movements /

who made maps by star so her folks could choose
between plantations   & promises of freedom /
who raised her children   & her children

& *all* of their children / rooms filled wall to wall
like blood filling heart chambers /
& even if you weren't named *woman* at birth /
never gave birth / or had to lay your firstborn
to rest far too soon /   you bear more

than nonfem flesh yields / you bear manacles
& barrel forward / you strike out & strike gold /
you strike fear & strike pose /

you are glorious as your feet when your song
plays / daily you divine ways to reclaim joy /
you are the best things about summer days /
sunlight warm as syrup / splashing up water
at sunset with someone you love /

& if I die before I wake / I pray goddess
my soul to take / forever and ever /
Blackfem

Record IV

new amerika (iv)

It's near midnight here in the fifth largest imperial city. Today a new emperor won the throne; fireworks line freeway lines like runway lights. What are we celebrating now? A six-wheeler pick-up truck—in the H-O-V lane—flys four flags: u.s., blue lives, confederate, and the fourth is spin-cycled by wind. I make sure to dress warm for the party. Still, it's so cold, we should have brought a heavy blanket set. You look gorgeous in honor of your joy, and I'm just glad the northwest drive is safe. There's no telling what kind of settlers live behind these gingerbread-brick neighborhood walls.

To cope, I smoke at night—ritual of my bloodline—I can't shape all my dreams (October days burned bright into the evening and I walked through doors half-awake). As I say good-bye to my friends I explain that I'm tired. There're more than two dozen cars around the block and I haven't seen anyone else in the street. We play Gucci Mane and Benny the Butcher; Blackmen having transmuted criminal to credible. *Property over People* says two-party liberals. *People over Property* plastered in my peers' windows.

It's past midnight in the fifth largest imperial city. Today an elect won both the popular and electoral vote. There's a pyrotechnic show of hope, a campaign term renewed. Most of the way I watch the road, and play Jhené with you.

Paradox

I was angry growing up; Baldwin says it best: *to be Black and conscious in amerika is to be in a constant state of rage.* I learned what school did not teach: Egypt's geographical location, lincoln's financial motivations for war, sharecropping, rock & roll's southern Black roots, experimentation on my folk without consent, terrorist attacks against our communities, assassinations to *prevent the rise of a (Black) "messiah"* and the f.b.i.'s covert operation against the Panthers, just to name a few. The real legacy pushed out allegiances, and pushed up rage and vengeance. A fictional character from my favorite anime, Sasuke Uchiha, became an outlet. Sasuke's clan are born with Sharingan—eyes that transform the color and shape of their irises, granting them incredible power. *If you know, you know,* but you don't need the mythology to understand the parallels.

The Sharingan belongs only to Sasuke's lineage. Many shinobi, motivated by greed, implant stolen eyes from living and deceased Uchiha, by surgery, or by hand. Sasuke obliterates one such thief, a high-ranking military official named Danzo. The truth, that Danzo ordered a genocide of the Uchiha, solidifies Sasuke's hatred for his nation, a place that eradicates and replicates the Uchiha for material gain. I too learn more, spurring on scorn: the prison industrial complex expansion, police murders of unarmed Blackmen, women, and children, Blacktranswomen's disproportionate rate of homicide, while popular culture plays dress up with Hip-Hop. Even Black teen angst sees metaphor. We *are* Uchiha. Freedom is a conspiracy against us, and without us—the capital and cultural wealth of this country—nation, flag, and all, would not exist.

* * *

If only it were as simple as you made it, Sasuke.
If only I could reach out with soft flesh hands
    & will the warrior bones of my ancestors
into a single pulverizing fist. If only I could look
at someone wearing the blood & labor of my people
    & bathe their skin in oil-black flames.

How did it feel to kill the murderer of your clan
    a dozen times over? Did you hear your cousins
calling from the afterlife? Crying? Cheering?
Was his blood thick & saline? What kind of crunch
    did his body make? like wood, bread,   ore?
When it was all over, were your eyes still red?

I won't be able to do what you did, Sasuke.
I would die in my world if I wasted any
important, old, avaricious roach of man.
I would be grateful to find such a man's name,
address & place of work. I would be grateful
to receive a weapon—explosive, traceless—
    with the means to activate it.
    I would be grateful to bear witness, freedom
    fireworks & skeletal rainfall. I would weep.
    I would vomit. I would laugh. I would know
    the price of vengeance, its sweet debt.
    Perhaps then, I could have eyes like yours.

Nobody

everybody wanna be Black / don't nobody wanna be *Black* /
don't nobody wanna lose breath / everybody want some long dreads /
don't nobody wanna dread cops / nightmarish *don't-shoot* ! gunshots /
don't nobody wanna forfeit / forget where their motherland is /

don't nobody wanna whip soap / it ain't pretty as the Migos /
don't nobody wanna be *Black* / they don't wanna live in handcuffs /
their world collapsing from depression like stellar core compression /
they don't wanna vanish / and become cold statistics / live life alight
in spite of / to die / and be rebranded cheap revolution / hung high
on pole signs for stature / or warnings for Blackfolk in the future /

everybody wanna stream Future / everybody wanna trap rap /
don't nobody wanna lose breath / don't nobody wanna lose self
to a jail cell / or Du Bois's mask / everybody want a fat ass /
big lips / smooth walk with a cool bop
don't nobody wanna lose breath /
don't nobody wanna lose breath / don't nobody wanna lose /

none of you

Love Letter

A love letter for avondale is a space opera starring me because I'm selfish and the universe revolves around me. Imagine a supermassive Blackboy made small, growing smaller with time, losing their gravitational pull during middle school and finding it downtown on a mic, pulling the Sun closer to the planet with their voice, a modern-day phaeton, no chariot—

nevermind. I'm important, but I'm not that important. Imagine a supermassive Black Family in a suburban home, one of two Black families on the block, but this one is mine, so it's *The* Black Family, *The* center of the universe. The brother and Sister are doing well. They listen to Erykah Badu before breakfast is done. They are trying to be Black but not too black and that's hard when you're so close to the Sun. *The* Black Family tried to be icarus and their wax melted—

nevermind. Imagine *The* supermassive Black Family is strong enough to hold a universe together. Imagine Father and Mother too at war for love. Imagine *The* supermassive Black Family collapsing. Imagine their whole universe gone. Keep that. avondale is gone. Where I visit childhood friends is a parallel universe. What once was home is now a wormhole leading to a Sun, but no supermassive Black anything. A love letter for avondale therefore cannot be; it is an unexplained phenomenon, a space opera, fiction.

CORPUS MEUM III

Momma said i ain't afraid of flight /
    since i was a knee-high seedling /
    bust my lip jumpin tween toilet & countertop /
        dive in my toy box / cut open on plastic /
        cousins run to Momma complainin /
            Aunt B / Sean's misbehavin again !
    in the backyard past sundown with gargoyles /
    eagle-height over islands / a canvas of blanket
    patches cover spring grass spun through a yard /
    these legs are ancient wings / fly into safer whens /

    these legs are ancient wings / fly into safer whens /
    patches cover spring grass spun through a yard /
    eagle-height over islands / a canvas of blanket
    in the backyard past sundown with gargoyles /
            Aunt B / Sean's misbehavin again !
        cousins run to Momma complainin /
        dive in my toy box / cut open on plastic /
    bust my lip jumpin tween toilet & countertop /
    since i was a knee-high seedling /
Momma said i ain't afraid of flight /

Consequence (DOOM Ode)

same game / ya can't reform 'em
    MF DOOM

born like this / into this sandbox where kids work until dirt is
wet enough for castles / antiBlack property powerkink / cops &
robbers gladiatorial social experiment /

born like this / into this playground plantation / where invaders
harvest vital organs from natives / collapsing corpse-fields /
surrender one's organic engines /

forced into this / no   consent consent consent
to calcify my divine sensitivities or brand me pater's peon / i do
not choose this mask hot-glued on my nose-bridge /

born with *the mask that grins and lies* / Dunbar's poem heaves
& sighs / prays to Christ / weeps & writhes / teardrops form
an ocean's tide /   witness ancestors deepsea dive some-
where below abysmal heights /   *remember*
whispers rays of light from suns & earths shimmering sky high /

born without the myths that tie my people to our flesh demise /
i remix legends to replace the histories denied descendants of
survivors who were stolen from their family's tribe /

i need not refrain / across homeworlds it's the same / appeals to nonBlack morality are zero-sum games / F*%K freeing half a kingdom / we'll free each enslaved human being !

Pokedéx Entry #238: Smoochum

after Marlin M. Jenkins

It always rocks its head slowly backwards and forwards as if it is trying to kiss someone.

In a world where coal-colored children are taught to fight and f*%k before they kiss, there was a bruise-hued child who loved their lips. This child kissed their shoulders and arms to fall asleep, and when their Sister wept, they kissed tears off her cheek. They kissed their Mother's moles and even their Father's stubble, they kissed and kissed and kissed until it got the child in trouble.

This child kissed another, of a complementary color, like bleach stains on a white T-shirt. Though they looked different, they swooned when lips locked; it was simple for the two, they were young and this was new. Still, in this world the lovebirds were not allowed to coo; bleach-brights could not love those of bruise-hues; those were just old, hard rules.

Still the child kept kissing and the other kissed back, smooching on buses, seated in the back, sneaking out of class, making out in the halls, even calling each other's homes to kiss through the phone. They couldn't get enough! The thrill, the rush! Lips on lips brought both children bliss. They promised to be there, to hold and caress. They promised to console, commune and confess.

With each passing day, the two were pushed away—heckled and hobbled—like horses in hay. The youthful could not grow as one, and the bruise-hued child spent summers slumped. I hear them search and search for porcelain partners, trying to remake the pain and passion felt when kissing *that* lover. I grieve for them, pray they heal and learn this wasn't their fault. Sooner than later, how else does one express love from the mouth?

In Our Dreams

*You're in my dreams / I can have anything and everything
I ever wanted*
Scott Ramon Seguro Mescudi, better known as KiD CuDi

you would bury yourself alive
& i would do the same /
that's why i sing   you /
us toy dolls of a child god
who does not know gentleness /

our minds are incendiary war /
a smokey siege of a stage
& yet you sung of the moon /
crooned for soft / wet light
to heal what cannot be seen /

desire cures nothing /
renders us unwhole / unseen /
what is it / the thing you want ?
the pursuit of happiness
is without   destination /
the brightest stars   die /
young & old / close & far /

i love you & love is maddening /
here i celebrate you & cannot
give blind /   unfit praise /
here i confront our ego /
the size   of our moon /
here i celebrate the maze
that is your mind's home /
here i render our pride mute /
asking us to wail once more /

i tire from writing for us /
our roots   in marijuana /
our hands   in women /
our voices   moaning /
obsessed with heaven
& marijuana
          & women /

we who /   malleable hearted /
find solace in sweet humming /
we who rap-sing our musings
dedicated to the sky / the moon /
our wounded / lonely / child self /
you taught me to be okay never
being okay / always being lost /

we who are no longer kids
must grow into gentle gods /
we who offer odes to all
except all our selves / dream
  who we want to be / all night

Record V

new amerika (v)

It's not hard to believe that this place—once prayed over by the original people who spat cactus wine onto the earth to call for rain—is now a military nest for warbirds and drone pilots. Beige buildings protrude from parched earth, and the rain is still protesting, refusing to fall, but those who make ritual of thirst and cleansing have been removed.

Instead my family is here, along with dozens of others, citizens playing our positions, taking orders, and adjusting to a climate that our ancestors do not remember. The first time I see heat haze, I think water is spilling across an asphalt road in ninety-five degree heat. Dad does not let up on the gas, and after passing through the road that shimmered misty and wet just seven seconds ago, I discover the desert's penchant for ghosts. The next time I see heat haze, an F-16C's engines blur the background behind it, clouding the vision of all who behold its flight. As a child, I thought it was cool. Now I wonder whose guardians help that raptor soar.

One may assume it's an easy question to answer; surely the progenitors of empire would aid a weapon's wings. But, whose empire is this? We built it, after all, on stolen land, for pale men who never have our consent. My parents, from the small rural south, and cold decaying north, brought my Sister and me here. Do our ancestors not want us raised, fed, and sheltered? Could they see a fighter jet preparing to take off, and gently lift the craft? Who are my ancestors, and would they recognize these advanced vehicles as radical reimaginings of sailing ships that snaked onto their shores?

Sometimes I wish that I could forget my ascendants, that they were not taken from me and thrown into the sea, atop branches of sycamore trees, or out of schoolhouse history. Does the land remember those who named it first? Sonoran earth cries for rain and receives only air force jetfuel.

record of Blackfolk in az

zero two / fourteen / nineteen twelve /
more than seventy years after the trail of tears /
I heard the first Blackwoman out here was a slave
of the Cherokee nation / pushed out by jackson /
heard she walked with her children back in
eighteen sixty eight / dragged over the land
we now call the u.s.a /   when she got here
she continued to serve /   I have no more words /

zero two / fourteen / nineteen twelve /
one century after / cotton fields still blooming
quietly on the far west side of the valley /
we pass white plants & Grandma goes silent /
her hands can't unstick sharp prickly-points formed
in summer harvest / the bolls / like a wetland's cactus /
bloodstained labor built capitals /   phoenix /
a state born post-war that protects confederates /

zero nine / twenty two / nineteen thirteen /
second street / colored school / renamed *Dunbar* /
Blackfolks are never called refugees but
we were stolen & thrown in these deserts /
we sing blues through global antiBlackness /
we wear the mask / forever spread across nations /
I hold to task every southwest historian /
you're half-assin   if you don't post our stories up /

zero two / fourteen / nineteen twelve /
Blackfolk (re)surviving world's ending & ending /
zero two / fourteen / nineteen twelve /
undocumented centuries of working in fields /
zero nine / twenty two / nineteen thirteen /
second street / colored school / renamed *Dunbar* /
I hold to task every southwest historian /
you're half-assin if you don't post Black stories up !

Debt

In this antiBlack era of Hip-Hop, streetwear has been hijacked by high-fashion, and Blackface boosts artists up the Billboard charts. Blackface minstrelsy remains the u.s.a.'s oldest, and most successful, form of entertainment.

Our music, now relegated, related, and reduced to *only* Hip-Hop, is both social currency and criminal culprit; our styles stolen by the likes of tekashi 69's and kid laroi's, reminiscent of Bo Diddley and Chuck Berry songs stolen by the beatles and elvis presley. In addition, we are not credited for our contributions to amerikan music; Black youth "bang" on instruments, or create "noise" on digital machines, white youth "play" in "punk" bands, or use technology to "innovate" sound.

Although Hip-Hop is both international and academic, public and private conversations on our culture disproportionately center twenty-something-year-old musicians accused of "mumbling" and "ruining the integrity" of Hip-Hop, like these rappers' grandpops couldn't have mumbled blues that made rock, folk, and pop. We don't discuss the consistent, generational tension among Blackfolk, or the constant reinvention of Hip-Hop by youth, or even the effects that pedestalling drug-dealer-entrepreneurship have on modern youth culture.

It is because of these critical, and potentially worsening conditions, that I write this poetic payment reminder, to every non-Black Hip-Hop fan, artist, and critic:

You cannot borrow our skin.
We are not accessories, slang words
or caged birds. We don't belong to anyone.
We name ourselves & speak in drums.
We use your cash to wipe our ass
& toss your precious   paper.

We do not own your stocks;
we did not steer your ships;
we did not crack your whips,
        yet we built all your shit.

We work, live, love & die,
you dare not look us in our eyes,
because you know we're human too
        & if you say we're human too
you'll have to treat us as human, too.

You cannot borrow my color.
I am not a commodity.
I am not a party song, cuss word
or caged bird. I belong to no one.
I name myself   wear myself.
You sell *me* to make *your* money.
You say I'm free, but *you still owe me.*

Touch

Britney Hiner is a blond girl I have a crush on in 3rd grade.
We're in recess. All the boys dash around the jungle gym like
race cars scattering across a track without boundaries: up the
middle under the bridge over the bars. We have infinite gas. We
go go go, running from Britney as she gropes with a forklift
hand, wanting to lift us & examine our parts like the under-
belly of race cars. I've been touched before & I said *no   stop
I don't like it*

I've been touched before & I said *no   stop   I don't like it*
I've been in someone's fist, delicate as a freshly picked flower
stem; I run from Britney but I want to be touched, want to see
myself in the lines of her open palm like marker on looseleaf
paper, I want to be felt, to grow fat as a pickle (I hate pickles)
I hate myself for saying *no   stop*
why didn't I like it? why didn't I want her hands   her hands
her hands

Britney chases all the boys
like a cop car in *Grand Theft Auto San Andreas*:
he steers his body around the jungle gym with Britney in hot
pursuit, up the middle under the bridge over the bars he revs
up the slide where Britney catches him. She unzips his pants.

He stopped, his feet are not moving, he likes it. Is this a game? Can he stop? Her hand is wrist deep down his jeans he laughs & she smiles a tight-lipped smile her hair's a broom covering a scarecrow's face & scarecrows mean STOP
she does not STOP   why did I want her to STOP

I park in neutral up the ramp by the slide; I'm hanging in the wind how I imagine bananas hang from trees, her hand is spidering across my zipper, curling like a spider's molt but her hand is clammy & cold, a towelette tapping me. I giggle. I like it.
I like it. Britney Hiner touched all the boys during recess & we liked it because boys are meant to be touched.   Boys   are meant to go.   Boys are meant to be touched.   I like it.

CORPUS MEUM IV

I'm aphrodite's child; my romances are wild. When I was twelve
I watched softcore for hours. *This is how to use a body; this is how
to take your power.* When my babysitter touched me, I bragged
to the boy who was our neighbor. Later, she let both of us touch
her. To put our hands beneath her clothes was a rite of passage,
a ritual meant to parse the penetrators from the penetrated. The
problem is, I still yearn to be full.

If I were lying you would know. Almost three decades living and
I smile wider than the bow of eros. I escape the state's battering
by traveling back to when I was a boy, back even further, before
I was a boy, when I bobbed in the baby brine of Momma's belly,
before I had a sex, before I even had a body. That's who I am:
the petaline pearl of a clam—producing too much light to be
identified. I am a grace, I am.

Reclamation

i had a septum & steel gauges / welded to the pit / super skinnys
Hot Topic tee / keys on my hip / izzy showed me DGD & i was
down with the shit / heard the rhythm & blues / Black soul
when the pick struck geetar / ragedrunk needin a fix of
hyperbolic rock & roll emos cooked up / our fav band sounded
like a gospel punk club   playin backup for a nu metal
rap act / their drummer had curly hair / pecan skin-tone /
but as hundreds parted a wall of death   my afro was alone /
    thankfully my niggas came ready to stomp on / we'll
    always be Hip-Hop /
    the membership lifelong / but something in my body
    knows /   here / i belong /
    i'm jumpin in the mosh like they're coverin my song !
        & negroes did make rock down south /
        not too long ago / after jazz /
        before rap's vertigo / when Ma Rainey
        & Little Richard sped up our traditions /
        impact for generations living today /
            but we are farmed like grapes on a vine /
            Big Mama Thornton's bellow super downsized
            into a chime that fits pale mouths without
            stress lines /
                even with our music gentrified &
                redlined /

we reflect joy & grief / each
genre / a branch
on a family tree / breakin open beats till
our truth is seen !

King of Nothing

i'm a King of diamonds / treasures i cannot take into another
life / i oversee my rock of rocks where my ancient parents died /
i was born a boy with fists full and gut empty / became a man
driven to riches by whatever means necessary /

i'm pushing a rolls-royce / i'm told the wealth of this land was
built by my ancestors /
i believe each purchase releases their phantoms / if buying one's
gravesite guides their flight home / eventually i will acquire loui-
siana / mississippi / alabama / georgia /

i guard this gold like dragonfire / i'm stressed out until i'm
smoked out / the only arm i cock back is a steel firearm
what have i become ? sold morality to afford vitality / my stom-
ach aches for laughter / butterflies /

is it true ? am i a sort of god ? youth worship from websites /
women and men open like petals for sunlight / whole wallets
handed to me like tithes / i had friends once / some died / oth-
ers i did in myself   if i am a god / are there more who may
redeem me ?

On Sight Contrapuntal

I need / right now
Kanye Omari West

I saw your tour.
Onstage before hundreds,
you sat atop an alabaster throne
of white women's flesh and bone,
a fever dream I've suffered alone,
martin margiela mask shimmering forever.
Blood diamonds masked as high art,
exes & women who appear in my dreams,
ontologically white as our capitol's columns,
double consciously Black as capital.
we understand grabbing a woman's neck,
pretending we're touching her soul.

    amerika is burning.
We hurt & hurt for the profit
    of brand name death,
the pale evil our ancestors warned us of,
    night & day, without rest.
Once, We said your name & meant
Let's give God praise, hallelujah,
    feast & hot bath,
once, your light was seen as a guide,
& now I see how much
    We played ourselves.
We propped you up   *too high.*

Record VI

in amerika

even the Reverend Dr. King died /
shotgun shells in Malcolm's sternum /
bullethole pelago of Fred Hampton's box spring /
no skittles or m&ms for Trayvon / just 9 millimeters

I too sing amerika /
tarentino's uncle tom snitching on Harriet Tubman /
kim k. hired to defend a survivor of police brutality /
    we pledge allegiance to these motherf*%kers /
        I pledge allegiance to napalm showers /
        and all lady liberty's pill bottles /
        one f.b.i. surveillance list /
        logging labor from double shifts /

sell me cotton & I'll spin cocaine /
front me cocaine & I'll flip Nike™ sneakers /
    buy me Nike™ sneakers & I'll jump like Air Jordan™
    far / far / away / where I can't be lynched /

I know genocide is written in the charter /
fineprint of the constitution reads /
the birth of a nation / *without her consent* /
starring marilyn monroe as ivanka trump /
      trafficked children playing Cherokee extras /
           am I too loud ? which do you prefer /
           machine-gun funk or machine-guns ?
           Black Panther Party or disney ?

where I live there's no concealed carry /
    we can settle this right now
    in this walmart parking lot /
    bring your crew / the u.k. & israel /
    tell russia we're playing nuclear roulette
        shadow-stained sidewalks in berlin /
    ask japanese descendants about hiroshima /
    ask me one more time about enslavement
        & civil rights & police /
    ask nicely & I won't shoot /
put your hands where I can see them !
I won't shoot / but if I find pages of history
ripped out & rewritten in the glovebox
of your company car / I'll call for backup /
pin you to the hood of a tax-payer's vehicle /
force my fellow officers to cover up my crime

    what do you think Eric Garner
    would have done if he had a gun
    in his waistband & not loose bills ?

    if you're wondering / yes / F*%K THE POLICE & the
    insurance companies & the corporations & the private
    prisons & the school systems & the u.s. departments of
    blah blah blah & the audience member who said *don't say*

amerika doesn't care about you because amerika watches from my smartphone camera & denies Mom's pay raise for 7 years & rips up Black neighborhoods to build Black museums / exhibits this poem on big / shiny / LCD tv screens & everyone livestreams & applauds & shouts encore ! encore ! encore !

you know what amerika wants ? more from the poor / from the brown / Black / more from the wars / you know what amerika doesn't want ?
    disruption /

R.T.C. (Right to Carry)

The right of the individual citizen to bear arms in defense of himself
or the State shall not be impaired, but nothing in this section shall
be construed as authorizing individuals or corporations to orga-
nize, maintain, or employ an armed body of men.

arizona constitution, article 2, section 26

you buy a gun to protect yourself. pawn shops run low on bul-
lets—better order online from reddit users. six months ago the
word *reddit* triggered you, now you're numb, and ready to punc-
ture a proud boy's bicep if need be. you tell yourself this and
you have never shot a gun. you most certainly have never shot
the hypothetical gun in your closet, although you hypothetically
point the pistol at your mirror from time to time, and pretend
hypothetical recoil rocks along your thin forearms. you've seen
enough movies, played enough games. if only war propaganda
could help you now.

tomorrow, the empire is electing a new leader; perhaps more
patrol stations will burn. you think crosses are more likely to
burn than surveillance vehicles and shopping malls, but you
dream. the elite have practically spelled these united settlements
of amerika; entire apparatuses exist to punish would-be "plun-
derers." a predatory state has invented a way to cage its poorest

and most vulnerable people, rendering your humanity illegitimate and tossing you in a violent cycle of use and reuse. people who look like you frighten imperials, but y'all aren't the ones who pirate land, slaughtering the original caretakers.

when you're asked which warlord you'll endorse, your answer changes depending on who's asking, but you're pretty firm in your beliefs. *I don't vote for men who commit crimes against humanity.* you're brave for saying this. braver still for saying this on-camera.

everyday you're afraid. when fear arrives, you know you can master it, but first you must master your nine millimeter. start there, breathe, and don't be afraid to fire warning shots.

* * *

you fire a ruger for the first time today. shells slingshot into the air, startling you. the first few shots shake your body from spine to heels. what nine millimeter bullets do to paper target hearts won't kill; what nine millimeter bullets do to human hearts won't heal. as you aim down the sights: steady your arms, hold your breath. this is only the beginning. fifty bullets spent on a monday morning, your lover and you one step closer to completing your list of life skills.

learn to shoot, cuz when your enemies come, they will already know how.

explorer's pack

I rap for the world that I want to see
cuz a Hip-Hop politic is stories & dreams /
no tellin how much time I got to breathe /
each song is a prayer / travel guide & seed

inna distant future / granddaughters break down bazookas
reusing tubes as   irrigation tools /
& boys wash babies / vegetables & fruits /
not asking for someone's pronouns   is rude /

teachers & staff are parents at our schools /
bootstrap narratives are no longer cool /
currency is worthless / community is fuel /
no human overworks other humans like mules /

plant life constricted every border wall /
facist party fanatics died in war /
the surviving apparatus paid Black reparations /
gender affirmation surgery is basic healthcare
in the ruins of united settlements /
a country long stolen is returned in peace
while once oppressed people rename ourselves /
each syllable sounds like a deep inhale /

I hear abolition will beget revolution
neither can happen without blood in the street /
they burned libraries   we share oral histories /
we're taught to wait for a prophet   we all could be /

I rap for the world that I want to see
cuz a Hip-Hop politic is stories & dreams /
no tellin how much time I got to breathe /
each song is a prayer / travel guide & seed

Battlefront

You play *Star Wars Battlefront*. It's a metaphor. In amerika, life is called a "game." Everytime you pick the rebels, you lose. It's a metaphor. Dad joined the air force straight out of highschool. The empire has a fleet of star destroyers, squads of death troopers, Darth Vader. The rebels have loud Wookies, kneehigh Ewoks, Darth Vader's orphan children. It's a metaphor. Dad was stationed in South Korea, shortly after enlisting. george lucas says the original series questions nixon's presidency, the war in Vietnam. george lucas ponders *how do democracies get turned into dictatorships?* He answers *democracies aren't overthrown; they're given away.* You counter: who is the resistance, and who is the superpower? But you already know. It's a metaphor. Your partner teaches you some amerikan history: napalm testing on Korea, incineration of homes—a country splintered in two, imperial bases on one side, the other side demonized for resistance. When you pick the empire, you win. This is not like the movies. In the movies, the empire loses, their experimental weapon is a Death Star, their grand, ranked army, a faceless cast of stormtroopers from across planetary systems.

You play *Star Wars Battlefront* with your friends, and you're the rebels. You point out that Wookies fight against enslavement in nearly all three trilogies. You say this makes them Black. Your friends laugh. Later, you discover that george lucas intended the Ewoks to be Vietnamese communists. This is not a metaphor. The empire, amerika, elite special forces wearing all black, reflective black armor like s.w.a.t. team shields. Darth Vader is voiced by a Blackman. This is not a metaphor. On May 4th, you count Black characters throughout the franchise, recalling five men and three women. Of the women, one is a voice actor, the other has a minor role in the last movie of the last trilogy, and the third plays a character loosely based on a woman of the Panther Party. This is not a metaphor. Of the men, one is *Star Wars'* first Black Jedi, who is killed off by bad writing. Another plays a character who is supposedly pansexual, in love with a droid. You smirk. Concepts of gender and sexuality barely apply to humans and animals, let alone robots.

Star Wars is a space opera. The series' first Black lead is underpaid and trolled online for his first movie. After four potential relationships, his character finishes the trilogy without glory, love, epiphany, the Force, not even a lightsaber. The only Asian heroine, a daughter of refugees fleeing amerika's war, is reduced to a minor role after the fandom expresses dislike and outrage on internet forums. She and the franchise's first Black lead never fully develop an onscreen romance. The fandom does not want a yellowBlack romance. The fandom does not want an empire of nuanced social class; the fandom does not want child slaves, the bourgeoisie, weapons dealers who sell to both imperials and rebels. The fandom wants their brunette protagonist and brunette antagonist to kiss. The fandom wants Jedi to overcome Sith, Light to overcome Dark, Hollywood faces to tighten bootstraps and win the damned war.

You and your friends play *Star Wars Battlefront*. Morals are made by those who win.

Mr. Popo (Erasure)

...anime does not try to accurately depict ethnicities or cultures but removes, simplifies, or blends them.

Alice Sparkly Kat, antiracist astrologer and storyteller

Mr. Popo ████████████████████ is a ███████ deity who serves as the ████████ Earth's Guardian. He ██ tends the grounds ████████████████████████ eternally as the gardener and caretaker, he can ███████████ travel anywhere in the world ████████████████████ by using █ magic ████.

███ Popo takes the form of a ██████████ humanoid. His ██ ████ ████ features include his ████████ dark complexion, red lips, and ██

██████████ a single tooth. He ████████████████ appears to be ████████████ the average Earthling. He ███████████ wears ███████████████ a range of emotions ████████ ████████████████████. His ███████████ style complements his ████ demeanor ████████████. Popo████████████ does not change over the ██████ years ████████████████, ████████████████████ and ████████████his agelessness results from his Otherworldly origins.

Mr. Popo

is   seen wearing

an aqua-colored jewel   on his forehead. He
sports a   gold hoop earring on each ear. On his
body, he wears a maroon-   gold-trimmed
vest   , as well as gold   bands on
his   arms.   His white
                              trousers wrap   around
his ankles   , he wears a pair of red slippers

.

Though he does not   physically age,

having served   the   Earth for hundreds
of years   as the
Guardian

, his vocation covers a wide variety of
areas, such as

training Earthlings and other creatures to
deal with   enemies of the planet

, taking over

if needed, and most importantly,
caring   . He
has a deep emotional bond with
time and will become incredibly depressed or worried
. He   tends to the ancient butterfly garden
he planted thousands of years ago, and enjoys the
simple things in life. He has a large amount of patience,
and
often attempts to calm people down.

He
greatly appreciates the natural world

█████ and █████████████████████████ commonly refers to himself in the third person. ████████████████████████

█ Popo speaks █████ with ████ sophisticated sentences, ████████████████ █ as a ████ ████████████ figure.

Mr. Popo was born in ███ Other World █████████ in the distant past████████████ , ████ sent to Earth to become the ████████████████████ Guardian of the planet. ████████ ████████████████ Popo was over 1,000 years old.

Hallie
after Morgan Parker

Every whitegirl I've ever loved was Hallie. I don't know why
I want her. She was cheer-team captain three years in a row. She
dated skater-drug-dealer Dan and cheated on him with baller-
drug-dealer Dashawn. Hallie's from the northside; her house is
on wigwam road. Hallie says she doesn't smoke but when she
gets out of Dan's Honda Accord, there's enough clouds to rain-
storm. In September, when the last rain of monsoon season hit,
Hallie's parents paid for a party bus to the homecoming ball. Her
dad's a sheriff, her brother's a marine, and her mom's a social
worker. Hallie choreographed a Hip-Hop dance to the newest
Lil Wayne song. She asked me for weed in AP history class.

Hallie is 5'6", brunette, green-eyed, and shaped like a gymnast.
White moon of my nigger sky. Sometimes I'd peak into the
glass of the gym door while the cheer squad rehearsed chants
(this was before I hurt my groin in half-pad practice and needed
muscle rehab). For Dashawn's Halloween + nineteenth birthday
party she was Gretchen from *Mean Girls*. I liked and unliked the
Facebook photos. Her page is mostly reposts from MTV, BET,
Hot 97, Chris Brown and Drake fan pages, and the lightskin
actor from *Grey's Anatomy*. She and I have spoken twice: the
time she asked who sells dimebags, and the time I rapped at
the talent show. Hallie smiled, *I didn't know you could rap*, and
walked out of the auditorium with her mini-me's.

I stopped following her on social media when we graduated. I visited for winter break one year, she served my Dad and me at the local sports grill. She still looked like an athlete, but she was tired, her eyes distant as an oasis past a stoplight. I also saw her ex, Dan, on my block the same week, standing in his garage. He invited me to a party on the westside, said his eighths were $30. I never went. The next morning, I went to the grocery store and saw him weighing turkey for a customer. I strode to avoid eye contact.

I checked out her social media again. I caught her Instagram live video, in a bedroom, presumably hers. Trinidad James blasted out a blue-tooth speaker setup on a black dresser. Hallie sang *nigga nigga nigga nigga nigga nigga nigga nigga nigga nigga nigga nigga nigga nigga* .

* * *

If I shall adore someone, it will be one who sees me holy.
If I shall adore someone,
                    it will be one who sees me wholly.

Iggy & Carti

We are now in a 21st-century post-partisan, post-racial society.
  Lou Dobbs

Iggy Azalea splits from boyfriend Playboi Carti...

Playboi Carti dresses as a vampire (and Kanye as a nondescript monster), and once in 2008 I told my friend who loves vampires about an idea I had for young adult vampire fiction. This was undoubtedly a response to the immense popularity of *Twilight*, but at the time I hated *Twilight* for no particular reason other than its enduring fans, who at my school were mostly nonBlack-girls (except for my Sister). Neither of these rappers need to cosplay fearsome creatures, they do so for persona, aesthetics, image, artistic choice. Deeper than character work, shock value, and experimentation, these Blackmen need not make themselves villains. They're already assumed to be such, by virtue of their condition, Blackness, a mark of social death, or curse of undeath. Carti and Ye are ascending the ranks of colorblind capitalism for a chance to cancel the sum of their skin. Talking to a bankteller any kind of way is how they conceive Blackskin without shame, but colorblind economics only means *all money is green*, which means *get money, fuck b*tch*s*, which also means *when he get on, he'll leave yo ass for a whitegirl.*

I have a strange relationship with whitegirls, as I imagine Carti and Ye to have. We've dedicated far too many lyrics and lines to the liminal space they hold as our lovers. I seem to float in and out of want with whitegirls, trying to prove haunting traumas wrong: that we can love each other from opposite sides of power—I'm not monstrous or undesirable, that love really can conquer all, just like whiteliberal revisions of Martin propagate—that I'm not (un)dead or ashamed.

Like most Blackboys consuming pop rap from 2004 to 2016 (the last half of bush jr.'s 8-year presidency, and the entire 8 of obama's), I wanted to be like Ye. I wanted to flip the vocals of children's choirs, Shirley Bassey, Ray Charles, and Curtis Mayfield. I wanted to say *the president don't care about Black people* in front of the whole nation. I wanted a lot of things. At that age, I had no clue how the world that shaped Ye's desires was working sick magic to shape my own—my friends and I claimed we didn't like Blackgirls. This was untrue, we did, but we said this because we saw how the opposite, dating a whitegirl, meant upward mobility in status, finances, and frankly, coolness. At that age, we had no clue how the world that would shape Carti's desires was sickening our own. At 15 years old, it did not cross my mind that I hated my reflection so much that mirrored walls left me wishing for freckles and lighter hair, I might as well not have produced a reflection at all; I was metaphorically like the Undead Count and his children of the night. I probably would have done anything to shapeshift into an amerikan boy, complete with a peacoat and that tall, dark, handsome countenance that somehow doesn't already describe me. Although I never read the series, I imagined edward cullen to be darker. Most nonBlackgirls at my school were team edward, but my Sister was team jacob, and at 15 years old, I could not see how whom I found to be desirable would affect her for life.

If Blackness is a condition of social death, then whiteness is one of humanness. Which would mean that: *nigger = shame*, and *white = pride*. What happens to the rich Black artist of the illegitimate amerikan empire is a sort of vampiric transformation, one's rebirth into an undead creature, occasionally born of a spellcaster's death-defying magic, but more commonly born after being bitten by some other, older fiend. Somehow, perhaps through distortions of abrahamic texts, *B(b)lack = demon* in western visual culture. This is a true shame, because nothing is more demonic than spanish / british / dutch / blue-eyed traders landing ashore, sailing some strange galleon you have, but likely haven't, seen before. (I say this, and I rebuke the nation, whom I won't specify; *if you know, you know*.) My point is, if *white = pride*, and pride was the first sin ever witnessed in our universe—having been sin's first begetting of demons, otherwise known as fallen angels (and no, you don't get to use my ode to Uzi against me)—then we can say that *white = pride = Lucifer's sin = demon*. Therefore, colorblind capitalists, whose wealth, like all wealth, is gathered by the exploitation of poor people, Black people, and migrant people, can never have as much power as (white) demon monarchs, who make niggas eternally deathless, thirsting for blood (monies). This system doesn't allow Blackness to be undone. Green cash can't change a color caste, but it can change a soul.

In a college course, I learned a little about how monsters are literary devices within medieval literature (think Chaucer and the Beowulf poet). Even their protagonists are a smidgen monstrous, altogether too clever, strong, gifted, or too lucky. In 2008 however, I knew monsters to be scary people-users, feeding off fear, mystery, and sometimes worse things like flesh, vitality. In 2008 I'd still much rather be a monster than myself, one with chaotic alignments of self, purpose, discipline, morality, and much, much more power than humanly possible. So in 2008 I imagined myself as the main vampire love-interest in my revision of young adult vampire fiction. Instead of reading or watching *Twilight* book one or movie one, I self-inserted as a 1,000-year-old bachelor, adept in dark arts, and of course, wooing whitegirls. My fantasy was sort of a sinister apotheosis through patriarchal domination, dressed just like Kanye at the 2008 BET awards—golden Murakami Jesus piece hanging from a spherical dookie rope, white BAPE wordmark graphic tee under a puffy, black Moncler down vest, shades up while onstage.

bell hooks calls it an *imperialist white supremacist capitalist patriarchy*, and Blackmen's imitation of it is a soul-sucking science. For those of my hue who desire such power, we metamorphose from emotionally sensitive to emotionally numb. We sanitize our brain for a sterile cool, cut our curls against their natural grain, cut out crying from our character altogether, and finally, reenact the violence acted upon us or around us, to establish dominance, but mostly to express the lack of. The masculinity of white oppressors is an affliction that necessitates intimacy absent of love, and harm of any magnitude without accountability. Their code of conduct might read like this:

1. Be not ephemeral, be everlasting, like stone, or death.
2. Be allergic to warmth, light; seek satisfaction in fissures.
3. You are a battlecruiser, an alpha leader, a medalled man.

* * *

There are little monsters, and big monsters, small evils and large evils. Not all undoing is the same. One bomb levels a church, another bomb levels a city. Same factories, same assembly lines, different sized craters. If Carti wears a Givenchy exclusive inspired by Nosferatu, how do we spot an occultist, oil heir manchild who's documenting his excitement from eating beating deerhearts? A sharper question: how long will Blackmen be caricatured scapegoats for the brutality of slaveowners, and slaveowner's descendants? Metaphor and violence do not exist in a vacuum; headlines about Carti sensationalize his stardom, his celebrity dates and girlfriends, but never the abuse he's inflicted to climb our social ladder. This young Blackman has shot at a young Blackwoman in a relationship with him. When asked about the incident in interviews, she's said *We were young, crazy; I lived in the hood. He would always shoot his gun off my balcony.*

Carti was raised in Fulton County, Georgia, a jurisdiction with a violent crime rate 10% higher than the national average, and a property crime rate that's 30% higher. He formed his identity in traumatic environments, and aspired to a violent expression of gender and sexuality not just for *survival*, but success (think *evolution*). To harm, and even kill, becomes more than his mask/masc, or rap persona, but his tools for both responding to, and navigating through, relationships and worlds. I ask, where's the line between performance and violence, in a society demanding the performance of lethality? Carti purchased a tank along with a massive estate, armored property to protect investments, residence, and property. There's no doubt that his interest in armored cars was affirmed, and likely advised, by mentor and collaborator Kanye West. Ye and Kim hire private firefighters after all, their entire neighborhood might employ cells of convicts to risk their lives extinguishing flames. Firefighters, police, prisons, military, all privatized industries and requirements for a sustainable ruling class.

Playboi Carti wears bloodred dreads, satin-black nailpolish, and genuine leather from shoulders to ankles. With crystal clear skin, and overabundant youth, he could be an actual vampire (according to *Twilight*), older than jewels that dance on his fingers and ears. The vampire is arguably the sexiest monster: severely tall, literally dangerous, brooding, and guaranteed to whisk away a wide-eyed virgin. These are most likely the reasons why I chose this monster to idealize; I didn't want to be anything close to the hellion I'm made out to be, here, in our world: grotesque, mischievous, and guilty.

These projections and harmful biases are a result of internalized antiBlackness reflected externally as misogynoir, but at the time, it was just what my friends and I shared on 3-way calls. I dreamt of being immortally irresistible, gorgeously goring, a dionysian villain whose vengeful crusade was to curse undeath upon nonmen not of my hue, simply because sexual conquest had been misconstrued as reparations and reclamation. This was all part of a grand, draconic lie. What I did not know was that I had no power because of my condition (being assigned male at birth gives me some proximity, but it's limited). My nonBlack lovers would always hold power over me, because my *Blackbody = shame* and there are no faculties within shame, only unmet needs. Instead, I was equally an object of pursuit, a badge, or bounty to be racked up and added to a collection. I wanted to be cool, sexy, impermeable as a spell cast by eros. My wishes eventually led me down a path of antiBlackness, assimilation, and addiction.

In 2008 I thought I was ahead of my time, and in 2020, one of Carti's captions reads *all My VAMPS sTAND uP ! X* on his IG song snippet, almost validating a 15-year-old Sean somewhere in a symmetric world. In our world, the short clip of new music says what I myself often feel: *this love don't feel how it felt when we started*—which makes sense, considering that we started high off Martin's frankendream, where Blackchildren hold hands with whitechildren atop symbolic hills, aglow by Georgia's dawn. This imagery falls mute when considering the state of the empire in the 2020s. Headed by a whiteman and Blackwoman, besieged by outbreak, waging antiBlack warfare at home and abroad, it doesn't matter one bit what a single Blackperson alone does in these united settlements. The message is sent clearly, again, and again. Equality cannot exist when a fraction of humankind murders, steals, and lies to fulfill their hunger for godhood.

Suit of Wands

will you come back home ?
i don't know where to go /
three bowls deep / i'm gone /
cigarette butts litter the lawn /

  the scent of you's a song
i can't forget the words to /
  your fingers in my palm
as sheets sink into whirlpools /
  we're let loose together
like children in (a)maze /
  graze my lips / kiss my face /
open our eyes / embrace /

we ask the cards how to grow /
they tell us *be patient & go /*
plant seeds / water / wait & sow /
new decisions replace the old /

our laughter is a starling sky /
  a flock wheeling in waves /
you believe choosing to leave
  is nothing more than fate /
when you return home
  i'll be courting healthiness /

day & night this well-lit room
　　　will witness daily discipline /

i can't just escape through smoke /
there's not enough trees unburnt /
pillowcase / blanket / porch step /
each is a site of our little deaths /

if this is my last life on Earth /
　　　let me be at my best /
　　　　　you push / pull / test / correct /

if this is my last life on Earth /
　　　then i will gladly
　　　synchronize our belly breath /

if this is my last life in flesh /
i'm honored　　to consult your deck /

CORPUS MEUM V (Afro)

I'm known in elementary school for having a fro because I hate getting haircuts. The barbershop is cold, crowded, and the seat is uncomfortable. When the clippers buzz in my ear I flinch like a bumblebee is biting my hairline, and yes, bumblebees don't bite, but if they could *that* would be how it feels to have the line above your forehead touched up with an electric razor. So I grow my hair out to defy and avoid the barbershop. What ends up happening is: my parents force me to go. I literally want to cry but I won't, especially around the men in the shop.

By 5th grade, my hair is massive, easily twice the size of my own head. Mom and Dad want me to get it cut but I don't want to succumb to the automatic pincers, the buzz-buzzing of black fluff that feels so good to touch. *You have too much dandruff,* Mom says. So I ask her how to not have dandruff. She says *boy, wash and grease your scalp!* She then demonstrates by washing my hair and greasing my scalp.

Washing is easy. I place my head underneath the kitchen faucet, sitting on my knees in a chair leaning reverse against the counter. She does the washing. Her fingers are explorers, parting the dense foliage of my fro, revealing dry earth. The water is a heavy rain before a monsoon that never quite becomes a monsoon. Next comes a towel that returns the land of my scalp to a healthy state of dampness. We go to the family room and I sit on the tile between her legs. *This won't work*, she says. So we go into her room and I sit on the hardwood as she sits on the bed. *Better*, she says.

In her room is where the magic happens. Grease is Vaseline for your head: a shiny bandage that melts after application, making one's hair soft. She parts my hair quickly with a comb. She applies the tawny goldshine with a single finger. One swipe, two swipes, three swipes, four. I laugh at how cool it feels, tickling me like a pet licking exposed parts of my skin. I feel good and I'm not itchy, or ashamed that I don't look like the military men, who wear low and bald fades. I look like me.

* * *

It may sound morbid, or (afro)pessimistic, but as an adult, I recognize my condition: socially dead says theorists, economically viable says markets, desirable says cultists. On nights when I'm unsure if waking up is worth my energy, I take care of my hair.

The actual application of grease is one of the last things I do. First I shower, a long, warm shower, in which I soak and scrub my hair. I have an eczema condition; my body is that of those ancestors who did not live in the sonoran southwest of Turtle Island.

Sometimes my hair needs two or three swishes just to rinse the flakes out. On those days, I turn the hot water down, to preserve the more sensitive skin on my crown. Outside the shower is where phase two begins. My hair holds water so well, I actually wonder if I am from a desert; it can take half an hour to dry my afro when it's freshly unbraided. While my curls are less runny than damp, I begin parting rows of curls, placing my finger into a near-empty container of Sulfur 8, swiping the thick amber elixir jam down my exposed scalp. The sensation is cooling, just like Mom's hands oiling my head.

Fortunately, I've been given this form: *corpus negrum*, 3/5s, incarcerated alien. Therefore I love me with all my might; I love fully, wholly, and holy as silent nights. Negro, meaning black, is designed to restrict, but Blackness abounds beyond loveless nights.

What It's Like To Be A Suburban Black Demiboy
after Patricia Smith

i try on lipstick / mascara / dresses /
and post pictures posing in Dad's bathroom /

i open my closet to decide which costume
will make me feel safe /

i remember a cop's pistol in my face
when I feel not Black enough /

i often feel not Black enough /
not masc enough / or fem enough /

i fall into the void that is my body /
i am charcoal and cul-de-sacs and poetry

and hours creating mythologies
of myself / documents of then and now /

with no sources to foresee my future /
i leave the skin i shed in the corner /

change my pronouns /
and dance /

Excerpts from *skinnyblk*

The Making of an Album & Play

In the fall of 2016, I began an artistic journey that would inevitably lead me here, to this page. My goal was to create something influenced by my friends and peers of the First Wave Hip Hop Theater program, housed by the University of Wisconsin-Madison. Although I had just graduated that summer, I wanted to fulfill a dream I'd had since arriving: to write, direct, and act in a one-person show for the program's festival, *Line Breaks*.

I embarked by completing a series of autobiographical prose poems and essays, which at the time was titled *Sunchild*. Although it was my creative baby for a season, it never came to full term, or alternatively, it was born under a new name, in a new when, and how. The title *skinnyblk* came to me after reflecting on the one major theme of the play: my body. I'll never forget: I was 18, fresh outta high school, and longboarding down the boardwalks of Venice Beach. My friends and I were on a trip to celebrate the end of 7 am car rides to Agua Fria, our alma mater, and attend Warped Tour 2011. As we zoomed, zipped, and weaved in between pedestrian crowds, we rolled past an unassuming whiteman, who promptly spun around as we passed, presumably to get a better look at our squad, and to say this ironic, iconic, and baffling statement, *whoa, skinnyBlacks*?!

My homies and I (minus one biracial whiteMexican boy) are, well, skinny and Black. It's just... our bodies, ya know? So we found this random stranger's comment to be hilarious and highly memorable. From that point onward, as a rapper, I nicknamed myself skinnyblack, in the tradition of Mos Def (now known as Yasiin Bey, who carries many good names, like Black Dante, Flaco Bey, Bezé, and of course, Pretty Flacko). The name stayed as that, a joke among friends, a silly, braggadocious bar, until I needed to reimagine my one-person play. I had discovered that theater, although my newest expressive passion and side-hustle, was fun, interactive, and interdisciplinary, but I could not create a damned thing without rap flavor and flare. That was it, then. I decided to not make a solo-play. Instead, I envisioned an ensemble one-act play, plus a choreographed, live rap & poetry album performance, made with and for my friends. I named it *skinnyblk*.

Shoutout my best friend, beatmaker, engineer, and DJ, Mic Maven. Shoutout my co-director and co-producer, Dr. Tamika Sanders. Shoutout the wonderfully skilled dancers: Raji Ganesan, Shelley Jackson, Justin Villalobos, and Niamey Thomas. Shoutout Ashley Hare, Jacinda Bullie, Mary Stephens, and Jennifer Linde, for providing institutional support. Shoutout my day-one best friend, Quincy Reams, for designing the flyers and cover. Shoutout the supporters and fans who donated to our gofundme. Lastly, shoutout everyone who helped revise the script, provide impromptu rehearsal space, worked tables and booths, performed at our special showcase, and just held it down for us. ♥ Enjoy!

(The following excerpts from the album *skinnyblk* by Sean Avery Medlin, available on all streaming services, appear differently in text format than audio.)

Power Ranger

(rapping)
Before I loved rap. Before I ran track. Before I got mad cuz they didn't text back. Before I bought sacks. Before I had sex. Before I played ball & shelled out my all.

Before I knew jail was different from prison. Before I knew race was made up by white men. Before I saw men with skin like me on tv long-tee gold teeth C.D...

I wore blue overalls & a red shirt. Nay-high. Always tugging on Mom's skirt. Fat cheeks. Smile like a melon slice. My hair, a flame in a fireplace. There was one thing that I did everyday. I was dedicated, nothing stood in my way. I knew the time of day & the channel. Every Saturday I was a Ranger!

X2 (sung by Carly Bates)
Go Go Go Power Rangers!
Newenewenewenewenewenewe!

Go Go Go Power Rangers
THE MIGHTY MORPHIN POWER RANGERS!

I was punching & kicking at the screen, battling Arachnofiend
& all the monsters at Lord Zedd's disposal! I squared up with
Rita Repulsa!

I was about it, y'all! Got ma Dinozord straight from Zordon, y'all!
But I never could decide which Ranger I was. Red was the coolest
cuz he had a sword. Blue had a lance that could shoot lightning
bolts! Black had an axe & looked most like me. Yellow had dag-
gers, I thought that was cool. But the Pink Ranger had a bow &
arrow &... her Dinozord was a pterodactyl! Can you visualize blue
skies from the cockpit of a dinosaur robot!? Mountains & cities
& oceans below!? Clouds underneath you like sheets on a bed?!
The wind, just a friend, aiding your wings?! But I couldn't be Pink
because, ya know, I was a boy...

(talking)
Like, you know what I mean. Blackboys are supposed to like
Blackboy things & I already learned what I'm supposed to be.

Before I joined the Rangers I had a ponytail. My Black hair
bobbed on my 1-year-old head cuz I got some Cherokee blood
on my Momma side as she pushed the cart & me down the food
aisle; traffic was mild but Mom got stopped by other shopping
moms & military wives sayin I was cute.

Then, Mom visits her family for a week. She tells Dad to part my
hair, grease, repeat. Dad tries once & he's not with it. He looks
at my hair, decides to cut it. Mom comes back & she's furious
but after that, haircuts become routine. I hate the cold chair, the
clippers buzzing.

3 years pass & my Sister's 12 months. She has a lot of hair &
well, I'm thinkin she needs a haircut because anytime my hair is
that long I get a haircut. So I take a pair of fingernail clippers

that look like scissors & snip snip snip till we look like twins. Mom walks in & she's furious & I'm grounded & I learn a lot the year my Sister turns 1. I learn that I'm too old to be carried. I learn that barbershops are for Blackboys. I learn that blue means boy & pink means girl.

So, considering my lessons, I should've liked the Blue Ranger, but he had a Triceratops & that shit can't fly. For Halloween one year I was the Red Ranger, which is fair cuz red was my favorite color, but inside, my heart belonged to Kimberly, the bow wielding pterodactyl piloting Pink Ranger! Every time Megazord assembled, her pterodactyl exploded from an active volcano & *that's* what I remember most from Saturdays, her pink & white mecha soaring over land.

Everybody said I was pretty with my hair & they mistook me for a girl & I used to think being a girl was a bad thing, yeah. Now I don't think it's bad at all, nah.

Tuxedo Mask

(talking over instrumental)
My friend & I used to play *Sailor Moon*; he'd be Sailor Moon, I'd
be Tuxedo Mask; we'd run shooting blasts from our open hands,
saving the whole solar system one Black barbeque at a time &
one time we were roleplaying the movie plot where Sailor Moon
dies using her powers to divert an asteroid & the only thing that
can bring her back to life was nectar from a life flower on the
lips of Tuxedo Mask & I didn't want the solar system to end,
so I kissed my friend in the tub he lay in, which was the closest
thing we could find that was like the coffin Sailor Moon lay in &
he smiled as he reached for my hand.

(singing)
X2
I'm your Tuxedo
Usagi Tsukino
anything for you
my rabbit of the moon

I'm your Tuxedo Mask
do anything you ask!
top-hat & psychic blast
I know I'm so badass

(rap-singing)
& you're so beautiful
moon-white & blue skirt twirl
late to your first hour
skip last hour gamer
two buns on your head
Princess Serenity
lunch dumpling eater
Silver Crystal searching
let's leave the evil
we'll play for the hi-score cuz

(singing)
X2
I'm your Tuxedo
Usagi Tsukino
anything for you
my rabbit of the moon

I'm your Tuxedo Mask
do anything you ask!
top-hat & psychic blast
I know I'm so badass

(rap-singing)
I'm your protector
& you're my true lover
I appear just in time
when you're in danger
I've dated plenty girls
none of em you
none of em royalty
no one eternal
you make my Black midnight

& your white full moon
I must be beautiful
when standing next to you

(singing)
X2
I'm your Tuxedo
Usagi Tsukino
anything for you
my rabbit of the moon

I'm your Tuxedo Mask
do anything you ask!
top-hat & psychic blast
I know I'm so badass

(talking)
My friend & I stopped roleplaying *Sailor Moon*. Maybe the anime got too old, maybe we got too old, maybe holding hands became unacceptable. At recess our classmate is crying. My friend puts his arm around her, whispers in her ear. He then lets her go & teaches me proper girl-consoling technique: Hold her. Stroke her hair. Ask her what's wrong. Tell her it'll be okay. I do all of this & she sobs harder, her brown hair sticking to my jacket. I wonder, what did I do wrong?

Hulk

(sing-talking)
I wish I was the Incredible Hulk
Then I could jump from sea to sea
I wish I was the Incredible Hulk
Then the bullies wouldn't fuck wit me
I wish I was the Incredible Hulk
Then I could slam dunk on my Dad
I wish I was the Incredible Hulk
Then I could get stronger, not sad

I wish I was the Incredible Hulk
Then I could crumble a cop car
I wish I was the Incredible Hulk
Then I could catch hel-i-cop-ters

I wish I was the Incredible Hulk
Then I could throw footballs real far
I wish I was the Incredible Hulk
Then I could be what real men are

X4
Harder than stone
Sword & a shield
Bringer of death!
I'd be mad alone

(talking)
I wish I was the Incredible Hulk
then I could be a patriarch
completely irresponsible
for all the destruction I cause
harder than stone
I'd be mad alone
bringer of death
I'd be mad, alone
my fist on the throne
of a distant planet
no longer skinnyblack
posing in the bathroom mirror
pretending the towel is a dress
questioning gender, sex,
attraction, the spectrum
I'd be ruling off rage
sick with muscles & veins
all this pain fattening
my neck, all this Black pain
shot through my fingertips
as I bend the nearest metal
into a pair of boxing gloves

I had a 24 karat gold
necklace Dad bought in Qatar
it had a boxing glove pendant
the necklace broke
while I was playing ball
I don't know why
I didn't take it off
it would have been
a few extra seconds
but ball was important

I mean I loved it
but ball was important

X2
& so was putting bodies on my belt

even though I never held
or fired a gun
I had to penetrate
dominate money-make
money-spend dominate
penetrate to be a Blackman
command the most power
or be commanded by those with
power, all Blackchildren
learn this early

(sing-talking)
X4
Harder than stone
Sword & a shield
Bringer of death
I'd be mad alone

Silver Surfer

(singing to instrumental)
I be dreamin dreamin dreamin
a world away
I be on a board hoverin
across starways
I be seein swellin suns right
before I turn
headin back to where I began:
the naught of space

I was man now my body's free
as meteors
I was color now my skin's like
silverlight
I was home now my home's farther
than I know
I was named now my name's
Silver Surfer

if I close my eyes long enough
I go away
if I think about my homeworld
I swear I'm there
if I think about my lover
I swear they're here

in the very place we began:
our paradise

I be dreamin dreamin dreamin
a world away
I be on a board hoverin
across starways
I be seein swellin suns right
before I turn
headin back to where I began:
the naught of space

X3
headin back to where I began:
the naught of space

X2
If I gather
all my cosmic
I can see home
I can go home

If I gather
all my cosmic
I can see love
I can be love

(rap-talking)
I wanna be like the Silver Surfer!
Coasting on solarwinds, dodging event horizons,
propelling past Suns toward the unknown
where stars blossom & fade like bruises.
I wanna be brilliant! I wanna be boy & more.
I wanna be my own hue,

I wanna reflect your image back at you,
I don't wanna be your gangster,
your worker your minstrel,
I wanna trace the letters of my name
across the black canvas of space like,
blaow! How you like me now.
It's the child from the Vall with the andro style
I be mild I be wild like a nimbus cloud
I be found in the crowds where the sayers shout
I be climbin out of me like an old molt
like an Orbweaver I be here in spring
then I build my web in the summertime
just to sit in the center while my body shine

I be free I be free like the Green Ranger
any spell on me I be breakin outta

I be breakin out, y'all
on my neck...
but it never stop me from feelin gorgeous.

I be free like I dipped from Galactus.
I be free like I fly around the atlas.
I be free like a bird out a birds-nest
or a cactus or a hat-trick.
I be free like I just bought a stickshift
I can drive anywhere in the u.s.a.
I be free how this country say
I be free like the word was my first name,   yeah.

My name means God is gracious
so I treat my body like somethin special.
Bein well received is somethin extra.
As long as I love me my world is stardust;

cuz I'm piped up & I could care less
I spent too much time shy & shrinkin
now I know that the sky's no limit
there's a hundred skies just like this
& all I want is to stand beneath one
& gun right past it.

demiboy

(rapping over instrumental)
X2
demiboy with the high cheekbones
& the self-love poems
come out on the stage
demiboy with the long rap songs
& the wide white smile
come out on the stage

demiboy do a dance
on a stage
if you joke
they will laugh
if you choke
they will snap

if you rap
they will nod their heads
down on every kick
if you sing
they will sing along
teach em your lyrics

you will stand
underneath a light

glowing electric
grab a stand
speak into the mic
gather your cosmic

demiboy do a dance
monologue about your pants
say a line bout cha parents
not a line about your ex
cept the one that you just said
keep your focus on yourself
tell em all about yo joy
tell em all about yo skin
tell em all how you feel inside, when you hold a pen
tell em all how you feel inside, when they call you him

X2
let them know, they do not hear you, even when they do
let them know, they do not see you, even when they do

demiboy reprise

(singing over instrumental)
I am dark & joy
I am glowing black
& caught in this whirlwind
of shit

I am dark & joy
I am glowing black
don't know where to go
but I know
that I am going to be!

(rap-singing over instrumental)
demiboy paint your nails
play your Gameboy
it don't matter
if they all call you boy

you know who you are
deep inside
the world never
labeled you right

stunt past every hater
in your black dress

stunt past every hater
in your girl jeans
who you are is still
your ancestor's dream
nothing here can steal
your androgyny

run around like a child
in a lawn
sing a song like a swan
on a lake
do a dance for yourself
till you faint
see a new purple hue
when you wake

you are soft-sweet flesh
gender is fake
you are your own best
life isn't great
take the pain
& confusion in stride
stay your course
& soon you'll arrive

even though your destination
is unknown, you will glow
you have grown
you're not alone, no X2

you will glow
& you have grown

We are dark & joy
We are glowin Black
& caught in this whirlwind
of shit

We are dark & joy
We are glowin Black
don't know where to go
but I know
that we are going to be

(talking)
Alive for ourselves
while sunshine still colors
our skin, let us shed names
we bear & did not construct
let us outgrow the privilege
& prison of stucco suburbia
let us praise our cheekbones
high as cathedral tapestries
let us grease our scalps
shimmy & two-step in peace

if we're queer, let us be
if we're weird, let us be
do not call us white
we are clearly Black
do not call us clearly Black
as if we are a stain
we are the same as dirt, seafloor
charcoal, oil, the canopy of night

we will change our pronouns
& you will adjust

we will love whomever we choose
& you will adjust
we are not respectable
we are definitely bangable
the star spangled banner
has given us nothing but reasons
to wear Black year-round
which, we prefer anyhow
Black is our best color

we belong here, we are here
& *nothing* will deny us again

Acknowledgements

Super special shoutout to the following family, friends, peers, and places, in no particular order (y'all know I can't rank the wonderful gifts y'all bring to my life)

Mom
my Sister
Dad
Clara Plenty
Clara Brown
Thelme Lee White
Jaiden Torrez
Quincy Reams
Ashley Thomas
Brandon "Mic Maven" Pink
Raji Ganesan
Anna Flores
Michael "CRASHprez" Penn II
Ashley Hare
William McCoy
Garrett Pauli
Debbie Devan
Megan Berry
Shantia Estes
Diani
Two Dollar Radio

Devin Killion
Eric Smith
Enrique "DJQ" Garcia Naranjo
Thiahera Nurse
Raquel Denis
Carly Bates
Erin Kong
Samuel "M A S U N O" Peña
Gretchen Carvajal
Malik "Qing Qoph" Muhammad
Palabras Bilingual Bookstore
The Reading Series
Wreckshop
Dr. Tamika Sanders
Tracey Pastor
F%*K IF I KNOW BOOKS
Nina Paz
Black Artist Reflections (B.A.Rs.)
Top Kat Studios
[nueBOX]
Mass Liberation AZ

Versions of the following poems have previously appeared in:

Write on Downtown: A Journal of Phoenix Creativity,
April 2020, digital:
    "Electronic"
    "Sun Valley" (now "Sun Valley (Shadowboxing)")
    "Iggy & Carti" (now "Iggy & Carti (Prelude)")

ChArt: Celebrating the Humanities Through Art,
March 2020, digital & print:
    "Mr. Popo" (now "Mr. Popo (Erasure)")
    "Hurricane (Storm gives a lecture on the Middle Passage)"
    "Genius" (now "Love Poem")

Alma-Nax:
    "Sun Valley" (now "Sun Valley (Shadowboxing)")
    "record of Blackfolk in az"

Indiscernibles in Arizona (The Virginia G. Piper Center for
Creative Writing at Arizona State University/Heritage Square
Foundation/Emancipation Arts LLC):
    "new amerika (v)"

References & Credits

The title of this collection, *808s & Otherworlds*, comes from the title of a 2008 Kanye West album *808s & Heartbreak*.

The opening quotations are from Danez Smith's "Why The Hood Bangs With Naruto," and Kanye West's "Say You Will."

The *new amerika* personal essay series is named after Erykah Badu's album series *New Amerykah*.

CORPUS MEUM is Latin for *my body*.

new amerika (i) 5
new amerika (i) contains lyrics from:
Erykah Badu. "Master Teacher." *New Amerykah Part One (4th World War)*, Universal Motown, 2008.

Mos Def. "Know That." *Black on Both Sides*, Rawkus/ Priority Records, 1999.

Common. "Dooinit." *Like Water for Chocolate*, MCA Records, 2000.

Iggy & Carti (prelude) 7
Iggy & Carti (Prelude) contains an epigraph paraphrased from the title of an article on Linda Ikeji's Blog.

Iggy & Carti (Prelude) also contains lyrics from Young Jeezy's U.S.D.A. "White Girl." *Cold Summer*, Corporate Thugz Entertainment/Def Jam Recordings, 2007.

Money is Temporary..11

Money Is Temporary contains a lyric from Drake. "I'm Upset." *Scorpion*, Cash Money Records/Republic Records/ Young Money Entertainment, 2018.

Hidden Cloud Remixed...13

Hidden Cloud Remixed contains lyrics from Kanye West. "Spaceship." *The College Dropout*, Roc-A-Fella Records/ Def Jam Recordings, 2004.

Free Pt. I...15

Free Pt. I contains lyrics from Kanye West. "Never Let Me Down." *The College Dropout*, Roc-A-Fella Records/ Def Jam Recordings, 2004.

new amerika (ii) 19

new amerika (ii) contains lyrics from:
50 Cent. "P. I.M.P." *Get Rich or Die Tryin'*, Shady Records/ Aftermath Entertainment/Interscope Records, 2003.

The Diplomats. "My Block (Freestyle)," from a 2003 episode of BET's *Rap City: Tha Basement*.

Jay-Z. "Roc Boys (And the Winner Is)..." *American Gangster*, Roc-A-Fella Records/Def Jam Recordings, 2007.

How To Make Trap Music 21

How To Make Trap Music contains rearranged titles of articles on 11Alive.com and Patch.com.

How To Make Trap Music also contains dialogue from the folktale *Anansi: How Stories Came to Earth*.

THUGLIFE Contrapuntal 22

THUGLIFE Contrapuntal contains several lyrics from 2Pac. "Ballad of a Dead Soulja." *Until the End of Time*, Amaru Entertainment/Death Row Records/Interscope Records, 2001.

THUGLIFE Contrapuntal is inspired by Tupac's acronym (or acrostic) T.H.U.G.L.I.F.E. (The Hate U Give Little Infants Fucks Everybody).

FURVA LUX (Black Light) 26
FURVA LUX (Black Light) is after John Milton's *Paradise Lost*.

Sun Valley (Shadowboxing) 28
Sun Valley (Shadowboxing) is after *The Great Migration: Indiscernibles in Arizona*, an exhibition by Clottee Hammons, creative director for Emancipation Arts, LLC, in collaboration with ASU's School of Human Evolution and Social Change.

Free Pt. II 32
Free Pt. II is after "Footnotes for Kanye" by Jasmine Mans.

Free Pt. II contains a lyric from Kanye West. "Power." *My Beautiful Dark Twisted Fantasy*, Roc-A-Fella Records/ Def Jam Recordings, 2010.

new amerika (iii) 37
new amerika (iii) contains lyrics from: Erykah Badu. "My People." *New Amerykah Part One (4th World War)*, Universal Motown, 2008.

Hurricane (Storm gives a lecture on the Middle Passage) 42
Hurricane is inspired by "The Deep," a song from clipping.,
an experimental Hip-Hop group.

Curse 45
Curse is inspired by *Naruto*, chapter 619: "A Clan Possessed
By Evil," pages 13-17.

Blackgirl Rock (Ode to My Sister) 46
Blackgirl Rock (Ode to My Sister) contains a sentence
inspired by dialogue from Toni Morrison's *Beloved*.

Paradox 54
Paradox borrows the line "if you know, you know" from
Pusha T. "If You Know You Know." *DAYTONA*, G.O.O.D.
Music/Def Jam Recordings, 2018.

Paradox cites articles from Narutopedia, including Sasuke
Uchiha, Uchiha, and Danzo.

Paradox also contains a quote from federal bureau of
investigations director j. edgar hoover, outlined in *goals for
cointelpro.*

Consequence (DOOM Ode) 59
Consequence (DOOM Ode) is inspired by MF DOOM's
"Cellz" (featuring Charles Bukowski).

Consequence (DOOM Ode) borrows from Charles
Bukowski's "Dinosauria, We."

Consequence (DOOM Ode) contains a line from the poem
"We Wear the Mask" by Paul Laurence Dunbar.

Pokedéx Entry #238: Smoochum 61
  Pokedéx Entry #238: Smoochum is after Marlin M. Jenkins'
  "Pokedéx Entry #778: Mimikyu," and cites Bulbapedia.

In Our Dreams 63
  In Our Dreams is after KiD CuDi's "In My Dreams."

Debt 71
  The ending of *Debt* borrows from Maya Angelou's *I Know
  Why the Caged Bird Sings*, and Paul Laurence Dunbar's
  "Sympathy."

Reclamation..76
  Reclamation is inspired by Yasiin Bey's (f.k.a. Mos Def's)
  "Rock N Roll."

On Sight Contrapuntal 79
  On Sight Contrapuntal is named after Kanye West's
  "On Sight."

  On Sight Contrapuntal contains a lyric from Kanye West.
  "New Slaves." *Yeezus*, Def Jam Recordings/Roc-A-Fella
  Records, 2013.

Battlefront 89
  Battlefront contains direct quotes from *Chicago Tribune*'s
  2005 interview with George Lucas: Caro, Mark. "'Star
  Wars' inadvertently hits too close to U.S.'s role." *Chicago
  Tribune*, May 18, 2005.

Mr. Popo (Erasure) 91
  The quote attributed to Alice Sparkly Kat comes from
  "Why White Queers Love 'Japan'" (May 21, 2020).

The text of *Mr. Popo (Erasure)* comes from the *Dragon Ball* Wiki article "Mr. Popo" (https://dragonball.fandom.com/wiki/Mr._Popo).

Hallie 94
Hallie is after Morgan Parker's "Matt."

Hallie contains lyrics from Trinidad James. "All Gold Everything." *Street Runnaz 71*, FUTURISTIC SWAGG ENT., 2014.

Iggy & Carti 96
Iggy & Carti borrows the line "if you know, you know" from Pusha T. "If You Know You Know." *DAYTONA*, G.O.O.D. Music/Def Jam Recordings, 2018.

Playboi Carti. "Over." *Whole Lotta Red*, Interscope Records/ AWGE Label, 2020.

Iggy & Carti contains lyrics from:
Playboi Carti. "Over." *Whole Lotta Red*, Interscope Records/ AWGE Label, 2020.

Kanye West. "Gold Digger." *Late Registration*, Roc-A-Fella Records/Def Jam Recordings, 2005.

Iggy & Carti also contains quotes from:
Kanye West from NBC Universal's 2005 "A Concert for Hurricane Relief."

Rubi Rose, singer, song-writer, and model, in a 2020 VladTV interview.

Additionally, the essay uses statistics of Fulton County, Georgia, from the Neighborhood Scout website.

What It's Like To Be A Suburban Black Demiboy 107
What It's Like To Be A Suburban Black Demiboy is after
Patricia Smith's "What It's Like To Be A Black Girl (for
those of you who aren't)."

Two Dollar Radio
Books too loud to Ignore

ALSO AVAILABLE Here are some other titles you might want to dig into.

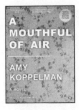

A MOUTHFUL OF AIR NOVEL AMY KOPPELMAN

← Now a major motion picture starring Amanda Seyfried.

→ "Koppelman's prose is as spare and powerful as poetry."
—Mindi Dickstein, *St. Petersburg Times/Tampa Bay Times*

COMPARED TO SEMINAL FEMINIST WORKS such as Charlotte Perkins Gilman's "The Yellow Wallpaper" and Sylvia Plath's *The Bell Jar*, *A Mouthful of Air* is a powerful, tragic statement on motherhood, family, and survival.

BORN INTO THIS STORIES ADAM THOMPSON

→ "With its wit, intelligence and restless exploration of the parameters of race and place, Thompson's debut collection is a welcome addition to the canon of Indigenous Australian writers."—Thuy On, *The Guardian*

→ "A compelling new voice, tough yet tender, from the heart of Aboriginal Tasmania." —Melissa Lucashenko, author of *Too Much Lip*

THE REMARKABLE STORIES IN Born into This are eye-opening, razor-sharp, and entertaining, often all at once.

A DOOR BEHIND A DOOR NOVEL YELENA MOSKOVICH

→ "A phantasmagoria about immigration, death, and queer desire... *A Door Behind a Door* feels psychologically resonant even when its events swing thoroughly into the realm of the mystifying and fantastic... As tempting as it is to slot Moskovich's fiction in with other works of the Soviet diaspora, the most salient feature of her work is its originality." —Kat Solomon, *Chicago Review of Books*

A NEW NOVEL FROM the author of *The Natashas* and *Virtuoso*.

NIGHT ROOMS ESSAYS GINA NUTT

← "A Most Anticipated Book of 2021" —*Refinery29, Thrillist, Book Riot, Lit Hub*

→ "Nutt has a knack for short, sharp lines that skip the brain and go straight to the heart." —Gabino Iglesias, NPR

NIGHT ROOMS IS A POETIC, INTIMATE collection of essays that weaves together fragmented images from horror films and cultural tropes to meditate on anxiety and depression, suicide, body image, identity, grief, and survival.

Thank you for supporting independent culture!
Feel good about yourself.

Books to read!

Now available at **TWODOLLARRADIO.com** or your favorite bookseller.

THE HARE NOVEL **MELANIE FINN**

→ "[A] brooding feminist thriller." —*New York Times*
→ "Finn has a gift for weaving existential and political concerns through tautly paced prose." —Molly Young, *Vulture*

AN ASTOUNDING NEW LITERARY THRILLER from a celebrated author at the height of her storytelling prowess, *The Hare* bravely considers a woman's inherent sense of obligation—sexual and emotional—to the male hierarchy.

A HISTORY OF MY BRIEF BODY
ESSAYS **BILLY-RAY BELCOURT**

← Lambda Literary Award, Finalist.
→ "Stunning... Happiness, this beautiful book says, is the ultimate act of resistance." —Michelle Hart, *O, The Oprah Magazine*

A BRAVE, RAW, AND fiercely intelligent collection of essays and vignettes on grief, colonial violence, joy, love, and queerness.

ALLIGATOR STORIES BY **DIMA ALZAYAT**

← PEN/Robert W. Bingham Award for Debut Short Story Collection, longlist.
← Swansea University Dylan Thomas Prize 2021, shortlist.

→ "A stellar debut... Alzayat manages to execute a short but thoughtful meditation on the spectrum of race in America from Jackson's presidency to present." —Colin Groundwater, *GQ*

THE AWARD-WINNING STORIES in Dima Alzayat's collection are luminous and tender, rich and relatable, chronicling a sense of displacement through everyday scenarios.

WHITEOUT CONDITIONS NOVEL BY **TARIQ SHAH**

→ "*Whiteout Conditions* is both disorienting and visceral, hilarious and heartbreaking." —Michael Welch, *Chicago Review of Books*

IN THE DEPTHS OF A BRUTAL Midwest winter, Ant rides with Vince through the falling snow to Ray's funeral, an event that has been accruing a sense of consequence. With a poet's sensibility, Shah navigates the murky responsibilities of adulthood, grief, toxic masculinity, and the tragedy of revenge in this haunting Midwestern noir.

SOME OF US ARE VERY HUNGRY NOW
ESSAYS BY **ANDRE PERRY**

← Best Books 2019: *Pop Matters*
→ "A complete, deep, satisfying read." —Gabino Iglesias, NPR

ANDRE PERRY'S DEBUT COLLECTION of personal essays travels from Washington DC to Iowa City to Hong Kong in search of both individual and national identity while displaying tenderness and a disarming honesty.